Road Scholar

Road Scholar

Coast to Coast

Late in the

Century

Andrei Codrescu

Photographs by

David Graham

Hyperion

New York

Grateful acknowledgment is given to the following: the poem "People of the Future" by Ted Berrigan from *So Going Around the Cities New & Selected Poems 1958–1979* © 1980 is reprinted here by permission of Blue Wind Press; "Sunflower Sutra" by Allen Ginsberg, originally published by City Lights Books, and "A Queen's Quest: Pilgrimage for Individuation" by Edith Wallace, published by Moon Bear Press, are each reprinted by permission of the author; and lines from *William Carlos Williams; Collected Poems 1909–1939 Vol. I,* copyright 1938 by New Directions, are reprinted by permission of New Directions Publishing Corporation.

Library of Congress Cataloging-in-Publication Data
Codrescu, Andrei
  Road scholar : coast to coast late in the century / Andrei
Codrescu, David Graham.
    p. cm.
  ISBN 0-7868-8081-3
    1. United States—Description and travel—1981–   2. United States—
Social life and customs—1971–   J. Codrescu, Andrei, 1946–
—Journeys—United States. L. Graham, David, 1952–   II. Title.
E169.O4C63   1993
917.304'928—dc20   92-38416
                                                         CIP

First Paperback Edition

10 9 8 7 6 5 4 3 2 1

FACING TITLE PAGE. *The Lady. She lets me look at her as long as I please.*

TO the longest sufferer of them all, *Alice*, who drove me everywhere in her car, and whose efforts to teach me how to drive came to naught; to my many friends over these past two decades from whom I mooched rides; to *Jeffrey Miller*, a great driver; to *Laura Rosenthal*, who let me drive her car; to *John Clark* for standing bravely by at the eleventh hour before I enrolled in Mr. Carney's Safe Driving School.

AND to the Crew of "Road Scholar": *Jean de Segonzac*, archetypal cameraman and French count, who, with typical aristocratic disregard, renounced his title to become an American, and who pursued the images in our film like a finely bred hunting dog, and then made me swear never to drive again after we finished shooting; to *Scott Breindel* and *Mark Roy*, our sound men, the first a fine repository of jokes, folk wisdom, and salty tales, the second a truly kind human being and a tireless uncomplaining driver; to *Chris Flannagan*, assistant camera, who danced behind Jean in perfect step, a good-natured and straightforward Irish American, who knows all about Jameson and Guinness; to *Dan "The Body" Klein*, whose boyish good looks earned him his monicker, and who used these looks to good advantage to hack through the people and paper jungles ahead; to *Ron Drenger*, young Frisbee champ, who tried to get me to bungee jump from a balloon, but was thwarted by my wisdom; to *Oren Alperstein*, who thought of bringing David Graham and me together; to *David Graham*, master of Eye, Wit and Energy; and, of course, to *Roger Weisberg*, who dreamt up and brought the whole project to fruition, Roger, who could spot a lonely phone in the middle of the desert like a coyote finding water, and who in stubbornness, perseverance, and faith brought everybody back alive, and a film, too.

—Andrei Codrescu

BOOKS are miracles that require guardian angels. Books with photographs seem to require more angels than most.

OF the angels that have visited me, I am most grateful for my newest angel, Xina, who, having just been born, will enjoy only the benefits of the published book, not my absences during its production. This is not to deny the angelic tolerance of my older daughter, Dory, and my wife, Jeannine, who were there for the absences that seemed to be infinite.

THE other guardian angels to whom I give thanks are Roger Weisberg and his band of loyal workers. Within that band, Mike DeWitt and Dan Klein seem to be the hardest-working guys in filmmaking.

I SHOULD clearly and loudly state that, without Roger, this book would have never happened. The idea and execution of the project began with his idea and the resulting film was the wave upon which the book rode.

IN THE category of itinerant angels, I would thank Orren Alperstein, who saw the link between Roger and me, previously, two strangers, and Tom Miller, who saw the potential of the book and saw it through. I'd also like to thank Faith Hamlin for bringing the book to Tom and keeping Roger, Andrei, and me together.

LASTLY I would like to thank my new and good friend and Transylvanian angel, Andrei Cordrescu. I thoroughly enjoyed his company.

—David Graham

Contents

Done with indoor complaints, libraries, querulous criticisms,
Strong and content I travel the open road.

Walt Whitman, "Song of the Open Road," 1881

Little by little we evolved the idea of getting a car. The only way to see
America is by automobile—that's what everybody says. It's not true, of
course, but it sounds wonderful. I had never owned a car, didn't know how
to drive one even. I wish now we had chosen a canoe instead.

Henry Miller, *The Air-Conditioned Nightmare,* 1945

So in America when the sun goes down and I sit on the old broken-down
river pier watching the long, long skies over New Jersey and sense all that
raw land that rolls in one unbelievable huge bulge over to the West Coast,
and all that road going, all the people dreaming in the immensity of it,
and in Iowa I know by now the children must be crying in the land where
they let the children cry, and tonight the stars'll be out, and don't you
know that God is Pooh Bear?

Jack Kerouac, *On the Road,* 1955

Where are we going, Walt Whitman? The doors close in an hour.
Which way does your beard point tonight? . . .
    Ah, dear father, graybeard, lonely old courage-teacher, what America did
you have when Charon quit poling his ferry and you got out on a smoking
bank and stood watching the boat disappear on the black waters of Lethe?

Allen Ginsberg, "A Supermarket in California," 1955

And now, next, it will be the deconstruction of the American Empire.

Lawrence Ferlinghetti, 1992

Introduction
Getting the Call

ONE day, in 1990, I got a call from Roger Weisberg in New York. Roger said he was a TV producer and was intrigued by my observations on the radio about American life. He was wondering if I would be interested in making a movie about driving through Florida and taking note of the bizarre roadside attractions that state abounds in. "I am interested," I said, "but for one thing . . . I don't drive." There was that pause, characteristic of most Americans faced with such a confession. In its own way, this revelation is as shocking as telling a Romanian you're a vegetarian, or disclosing an odd sexual preference to your parents. But Roger recovered quickly. "Would you *like* to drive?" he asked.

I felt as if I were at a crossroads. Would I like to drive? Would a fish like to fly? Would a child like to be a grownup? Would an elephant like to be a swan? Was it a matter of *wanting to*, or was it more like an impossible cross-species dream, a magical transformation? "Well, no . . ." I said. "I've come this far walking, why spoil a good thing?"

Two years later Roger called back. I have since learned that once an idea has taken hold in his mind Roger will not rest until he knows for sure whether it works or not. It's a phenomenal quality, especially astonishing to one like me who is willing to entertain another thought immediately if the first thought proves somehow fallible. This time, he had a suggestion. "How about us paying for driving lessons, filming them, and making it a part of the movie?"

I told him I would think about it, but that if by some miraculous process I actually learned how to drive, we should go way beyond Florida's roadside attractions. We should make a movie about America, a driver's America, *my* driver's America. Although I had lived for one-quarter of a century in America and considered myself at least as American as Goldwyn and Mayer, the European Jews who invented Hollywood, and a lot more American than Henry Kissinger, I did not know America like most Americans. Mine was a pedestrian's America, an America of big cities with good public transportation and walkable streets. What I knew from a car was from the passenger's side, a position that was subject to the whims of the driver. I did not know the driver's America that Jack Kerouac wrote about in *On the Road,* the America of forgotten country roads and lonely highways.

There was something vast and scary too in the jillions of driving-and-heartbreak songs that poured out of every radio. I wasn't sure I wanted to know all that.

But something there was in me that liked the thought, as Robert Frost never said. Here was a chance for me to transform myself once more, to begin again. I love being born again, and I practice it. It's my passion, also my *métier,* my specialty. Changing names, places of residence, body shapes, opinions . . . what endless delight. America was set up for this kind of thing, a vast stage for projecting images of self that Europe had made impossible.

I went to the WNET television studios where Roger's company, Public Policy Productions, is located, in the tiny rooms of a former transient hotel. Roger Weisberg's walls were festooned with awards for serious documentaries. His intense, wiry person communicated a purposeful and pointed sense of things. Young, bright-looking people walked in and out with memos and faxes. I had the sudden feeling that we were from different planets. On his planet, facts, figures, and a directed sense of social outrage ruled. It was a *rational* planet. Roger made documentary films about the health-care crisis, clear-cut statements filled with moral outrage calculated to induce a change in public policy. (They did.) I admired this sort of thing. On my planet, however, the twilight of ambiguity reigned. My landscapes were paradoxical, my motives obscure until examined, my expectations nonexistent, my outlook ironic and pessimistic (until proven otherwise), and my hatred of the seeming sturdiness of facts a lifelong struggle.

Yes, I might be willing to drive but there was no good reason to. From a health-care perspective, I probably ought not to. Furthermore, I did not want to drive to places everybody else drove to; if I was going to do it I would go to places that Americans never see on television or hear mentioned in their newspapers. And furthermost, I expected to find nothing in those places, partly because there would be little time to discover anything genuine, and partly because I never found anything of interest deliberately; the best discoveries of my life have been by accident. If anything was to come of my journey, it would be like that, by accident (maybe even *from* an accident, God forbid, knock on wood!), certainly not through the sort of careful research Roger specialized in. I mean, people may discover things while driving, but who ever discovered anything while making a driving *movie*?

Also, on my planet, it was strictly forbidden to use language the way TV—from ABC to PBS—uses it, which is to say like a dead body being dragged along a wet floor by a Nazi. I wrote a book called *The Disappearance of the Outside*, in which I detailed the many ways in which thinking has been replaced by television programming in our time. I believe that by the end of the century no one will be able to distinguish between real people and TV people. Who is the real person: Dan Quayle or Murphy Brown? There are good reasons why I never watch TV—besides the main one, which is that it's a death trap for the American mind.

To these objections and others like them, Roger countered that it would be an experience to remember nonetheless, and then offered me a ridiculously small amount of money that was, however, more than my poetry had earned me in a lifetime of practicing its dangerous pinturns.*

I went home confused and intrigued, one of my favorite mental states. During the week that Roger's proposal was beginning to germinate in my mudlike mind, I received another telephone call. The producers of a travel movie about buses, trains, and airplanes were wondering if I would be interested in narrating the sights from aboard these conveyances.

Nineteen ninety-one was clearly my year for Telephone Calls from the Movies. At the beginning of that fateful year, I received three calls in a row from Hollywood. The first one was from a famous producer who wanted me to write a movie using my book about the Romanian revolution of 1989. "The revolution would be a background," he explained, "for a love story between two journalists." "Julia Roberts and

---

*If there is anything more dangerous than driving, it's poetry: only parts of California Highway One compare with it.

Dustin Hoffman?" I asked. "Precisely!" came the enthusiastic reply. "Didn't they make that already? *The Year of Living Dangerously*?" I asked. "Precisely!" came the unfailingly enthusiastic reply. The second call came from someone who wanted to make a movie very much like the one the first call described, but in addition there would be a little vampirism in this one because Transylvania was in Romania. "You mean, Communist vampires prey on collective farm maidens to the point where they must be overthrown?" I asked. "Precisely!" came the satisfied reply. I could hear the smooth flow of a gold-nibbed Parker across a glossy napkin.

The third call was from an extremely powerful Hollywood mogul, who declared himself impressed by one of my observations on the radio. "If you see something in the newspaper," the mogul said, "that can be developed into a script . . . I'd like to see it." I told him that I had filled books with these sorts of observations and that I would send them to him. There was a brief, imperceptibly appalled pause. Clearly that was a faux pas. It was. I sent the man books, but heard nothing from him. I called back. "To tell you the truth," he said, "your material is too elevated for the marketplace." That was news to me. I should have sent him my poetry. That would show him "elevated." In fact, I don't think he even read those books. The most book anybody in Hollywood reads is the menu in a fancy restaurant. (In all fairness, some of these menus are pretty thick, and there are a lot of foreign words!)

About ten years ago I went with my wife's cousin Phil to the house of a hairdresser in Hollywood to buy some pot. There was a very tony party going on in the hairdresser's living room. While Phil and the host did business by the garage, I wandered into the party and noted that an expensively dressed dwarf was enthroned in the middle of the room with an adoring coterie arrayed about his Guccis. I walked up to him and asked him: "What do you do?," an act of *lèse-majesté* that silenced and horrified the entourage. In a high-pitched whiny voice the dwarf said haughtily: "I'm the houseboy of the president of Paramount Pictures!" I liked that since I had just had a book published by Pocket Books, a company owned by Paramount. "How do you get a book made into a movie?" I quizzed the dwarf. "We don't make movies from books," he replied icily, "we make books from movies." That was a lesson. Ten years later, things are even more like that.

Roger Weisberg was quite different. He not only read books, he read *mine.* The producers of the buses, trains and airplanes movie were pretty serious types, too. They had also made documentaries about serious social concerns, including a widely acclaimed picture about AIDS. I still had no idea what all these sober folks wanted from me. But there was one radical difference between my two suitors. If I made observations from buses, trains, and airplanes I wouldn't have to drive at all. I wouldn't have to learn—a thought that gave me chills—and I wouldn't have to pass a test—another cold-sweat-causing idea. On the other hand, there would be little new for me in seeing America from buses, trains, and planes. I had been commuting from New Orleans to Baton Rouge, where I teach, by Greyhound bus for years. I have taken Amtrak from coast to coast, and I fly more planes than I care to think about. I know the people who ride the buses well, and one day I would love to write about them. The train is but a nostalgic throwback. Air travelers are busy, distracted, and uniformly depressing.

I flew to San Francisco to meet with the public-transport producers. We had lunch in a posh restaurant on Market Street, where we were handed a separate menu for water. They had fifty different kinds of water. They also had thirty different kinds of oysters, each of which cost between three and six dollars. The six-dollar oyster was the tiniest of them all. The smallest pearl would have found no haven in its flesh. The lunch was nice. The producers were nice. We didn't get along. I commented on the size of the oysters. I ordered bourbon instead of water. I smoked a cigarette. They decided to make their movie without a narrator.

I didn't hear from Roger Weisberg for months. I tried to forget about the whole idea. Clearly I wasn't *meant* to drive. But something had been set in motion. I began to examine my nondriving self.

Road Scholar

Carless in America

ALL my life I had two claims to fame: I was born in Transylvania and I didn't drive a car.

The first fact made people naturally assume that I didn't *need* to drive because I could always use bats. I can, but it's a hassle to harness the bats every time you need a quart of milk. Try parking bats outside the Safeway! My life would have been much simpler, I think, if I had learned how to drive when I came to America. An American without a car is a sick creature, a snail that has lost its shell.* Living without a car is the worst form of destitution, more shameful by far than not having a home. A carless person is a stationary object, a prisoner, not really a grownup. A homeless person, by contrast, may be an adventurer, a vagabond, a lover of the open sky. The only form of identification an American needs is a driver's license.

Time and time again I stood humiliated before a bank clerk who would not admit to my existence because a passport meant nothing to her. Over and over I've had to prove my existence to petty clerks and policemen for whom there was only one valid form of ID. Driven to despair, I wrote my first autobiography, *The Life and Times of an Involuntary Genius*, at age twenty-three for the sole reason of having my picture on the cover. Whenever a banker asked to see "some identification," I pulled the book from my mirrored Peruvian bag and pointed to the cover. More often than not, it was not enough. "What we mean is," the flustered interpreters of rules and upholders of reality would insist, "we want to see some *proper* ID!" Books have never been proper to those in charge of upholding the status quo.

*That's why one of the biggest gas companies is called Shell: it feeds Americans' exoskeletons.

ONE very late night in California my friend Jeffrey Miller and I got lost on a country road somewhere above the Pacific Ocean. The sky was pierced by so many stars we thought we were on a cosmic stage with the ocean roaring below us. We stopped because we were tired and awed. Suddenly, the lights of something unearthly and huge were upon us. It was a California Highway Patrol cruiser, its blue light flashing. Jeff stopped slowly, as if he were reluctant to surrender to the intense light, which might be an alien craft. The officer asked Jeff for his ID, which my friend fished with some difficulty either from the depths of his fascinating glove compartment, which was his portable office, or from one of his pockets, which was equally cluttered with napkins full of poetry, pencil nubs, lucky stones, and, undoubtedly, Ritz crackers in case of shipwreck. Jeffrey believed every journey was final, and that one must be prepared.

The officer then turned to me. "Your license!" "I don't drive," I said. He heard that. He also heard the foreign "r" in the word "drive," and was alerted to the possibility of a potential illegal alien. I pulled out my book. "I wrote this. See, that's my picture!" The cop took the book back to his cruiser and started reading. He read and read. Eons passed. The stars in the sky changed. Jeff and I slept and woke, grew old, died, and came back. At long last, the officer returned from the deeps of time, and tapped my face on the cover with a thoughtful trigger finger. "Anybody can fake a pitcher like this!" he said. "If they could," I argued wearily, "would they bother to write a book to go with it?" "It's OK," he said, *"this time!"* Well, it was OK that time, and Jeff and I went on our way. I immediately wrote another autobiography, for that California cop. In that book, called *In America's Shoes,* which also sports my face on the cover, I told the above story—just in case we met again.

My adventures in the land of those without drivers' IDs would fill several books. Lost souls live in that world: illegal aliens, space aliens, the crazy, the stubborn, handicapped pedestrians of every stripe. The truth is that an American without a driver's license doesn't have an identity.

I TRIED to learn. Three times. The first time was in 1967, in my wife Alice's old Ford station wagon, a frightening vehicle that would have been rejected by Rent-a-Wreck if Rent-a-Wreck had been around in 1967. Our friend Jan Herman, who gave it to her, didn't think that the clunker would last twenty-four hours. It did in fact last almost a year, even after it had its tires slashed on the Lower East Side of New York, its windows broken in Detroit during the '67 riots, and a garbage bag dropped on it from the fifth floor of a tenement in Harrisburg, Pennsylvania. The thing was made to suffer and withstand disasters: if it had been human it would have been a saint. I was still a brand-new American then, filled with the desire to become motorized. We headed for the Palisades of New Jersey, those sheer cliffs just outside of Manhattan, on a beautiful sunny day. Alice showed me the brake, the gas pedal, and the wheel, and then settled back confidently as I drove straight to the edge of the precipice—and would have driven over if she hadn't quicker than Zorro speared the brake.

The second time I tried was in a church parking lot in California on a Tuesday in 1973. There were no cars in the lot except the reverend's black Oldsmobile neatly stashed in the shadow of a walnut by the church wall. I did great that time. I turned, I backed out, I revved, and then I headed helplessly for the reverend's car and bashed the door on the driver's side. I think I was possessed. It's the only explanation. The devil likes cars and is especially fond of new drivers. Give him one in a church parking lot and he has an orgasm.

The third time I actually drove. In 1975, Alice's yellow Vega was the snazziest car in Monte Rio, California, a little town filled with shady people where the population thought that food stamps were the official U.S. currency. The Vega, of course, was not really a car but a lemon, a real piece of American junk, probably *the* piece of junk that finally got everybody buying Japanese cars. Anyway, I got in it and drove out of Monte Rio on a lovely curving back road following a stream on a beautiful morning, and I was actually *enjoying* it! The leaves made pretty patterns with light on the windshield, the world was peaceful and playful, and I drove right into the stream. I had gotten so confident I forgot to steer.

It was at that point that I decided cars and I were not meant for each other. Neither concentration nor relaxation, neither will nor dreaming worked for me. I was doomed to be what I had always—happily—been: a pedestrian.

Alternative Transports

I LEFT Transylvania by air in 1965 and got to America in 1966 (it was a long flight!) at just about the time that my generation was piling into VW vans and striking out for the Wild West (again). I went along and lived in a lot of places, among them Detroit, New York, Chicago, and San Francisco. Now I live in New Orleans. I rode along to all these places, the passenger *par excellence*. I was *The* Passenger. I knew exactly what was expected of me. I knew how to entertain at just the right speed. I was not a backseat driver, and my remarks were geared to the driver's moods like a violin to a heartbreak.

Being The Passenger for years was immensely beneficial. At the end of a party, for instance, while my unsteady contemporaries headed for their many cars, I could pick and choose my ride. If I picked the most beautiful woman leaving, alone like everyone else, in her isolated bubble of plastic and glass, can anyone blame me? As folks headed for the sadness of the parking lot, each one to his or her own car, I felt the loneliness. I was a most welcome passenger. I was the one you could give a ride to. I was also the one left, occasionally, standing by the side of the road. Of these occasions I rarely speak though I have some really dark-night-of-the-soul memories that I *could* reveal someday if I find the right therapist.

There were also delicate situations in certain rude places out West where it got rough. To some of them dudes drinking dusty beer in the desert, a nondriving man was a distinct freak of nature, a thing created for cruel entertainment, something effeminate and unnatural made to be prodded with sticks. I had to brave their ridicule and incomprehension now and then, it's true, but it was a small price to pay for the pleasure of being the Consummate Passenger and the Perfect Pedestrian. Being both carless and unidentifiable I began to identify with my Saintly Condition, which called for capitals. One does not really suffer unless one Suffers.

Later, in the seventies, when it became fashionable to not drive because of the environmental horror that is the car, I could have (and occasionally did) claim I was taking a stand. In my own way I was. I walked everywhere and took public transportation when I couldn't mooch a ride. In truth, it was something other than a stand that underlay my handicap, namely:

MY MOTHER

WHEN my mother came to America at age forty-four, she got her driver's license and a huge used Pontiac. Instantly, she became a very great menace, one of those little ladies who can barely see over the dashboard. She never drove over thirty miles an hour, and it is only by the grace of God that many drivers in her vicinity are alive today. One of the most harrowing experiences of my life was when I went to visit her with my son Tristan at the time she was trying to buy a new car. After intimidating a huge, self-confident salesman who became a mass of jelly before her boundless ignorance and energetic suspicion, she drove this used Cadillac out of the dealership onto the freeways of Florida with my son and me inside. She had no idea what most of the buttons and gears were for because she was used to her old car. While complaining the whole time that she'd been swindled and that the car didn't work, she drove in reverse, she made U-turns on the expressway, and she missed her exits. My son and I were reduced to raw nerves by the experience. I'm sure she gave her grandson a permanent complex. We went back to the dealership eight times. She raged about the defective machine but each time she allowed herself to be persuaded there was nothing wrong with the car and tried again. The sixth time we went back, the huge salesman hid from her in a bathroom and submitted his tearful resignation through the door. The owner of the company had to be called in to personally reassure my mother that the car was fine.

In the end, she returned the Cadillac anyway, and got her old car back. The Pontiac, even though it didn't work very well, was her friend. She was proud of it. For ten years she had sent our relatives in Romania pictures of herself with the car: Mother with her hand on the roof of her car. Mother at the wheel. Mother sitting on the hood of her car. For about a year after she learned to drive, Mother had a big sign in the back window: CAREFUL! BEGINNER! Fortunately, people took her at her word and avoided her. A fierce, tiny human being with a bright red permanent barely visible above the dash of her American machine, she was like a determined time traveler who had come from the

Middle Ages to experience the modern world, and experience it she did. Never mind the terror she spread around her on freeways and streets. In spite of it, I admired her courage. It takes guts to come to a foreign land in your middle age and become one of the armored natives.

Curiously enough, my father, who divorced my mother when I was only six months old, was a superdriver. He drove so fast on the cobblestone streets of my childhood my neighbors had no pets.

MY FATHER

MY father's big black Packard scared our neighbors in Sibiu, Romania. There were only six cars in town and my father had one. He also wore a black leather jacket. When he passed people bowed their heads in fear and whispered. When he was gone, they spat and crossed themselves. In those days, at the height of Stalinist terror, the man in the car was the one who came to take you away: he took you away in his car and you never came back again.

My father took me in his car but he always brought me back to my mother on Sunday night. Every Saturday, from age six to nine, I got in my father's black car to the pointed envy and fear of our neighbors, and took off to visit his girlfriends. I waited for him in the car, behind the wheel, not moving, while my father was in a building somewhere, and fantasized about driving the black car. When my father came back, smelling of cheap cologne and a strange carnal odor that took me years to identify, I was exhausted. I had driven thousands of miles through the crooked streets of our medieval burg and I had received the frightened tribute of every citizen who had ever slighted me in the least. I had also magnanimously given rides to every person who had ever been nice to me. My father never suspected a thing because I was sure to set back the odometer. I was such a good imaginary driver, I saw no point in actually driving. But one time I did drive. My father had left the key in the ignition. I got behind the wheel, released the brake, and rolled straight into the window of a hat store. When my father came back I was shaking helplessly in the driver's seat under a mountain of hats. He never left the key in after that. After that, I never wore a hat.

Cars were as rare as swans in Sibiu. As they navigated the twisted streets, the pedestrians watched them with the same kind of dread with which they had once watched the carriages of Transylvanian nobles. The cars of the fifties, like the coaches of the sixteenth century, stopped for no one. The plebes took the bus or rode honest bicycles, which had come through the war. Waiting for the bus in the rain, I would watch the depressing river of bicycles streaming to work, and I could see myself on the back of a swan. My white bird would glide over the gray river of bikes, then soar over the towers of the Teutsch cathedral, skirt the silvery roofs of Sibiu and land in the schoolyard just as the bell rang.

I rode a swan to school (though most of my Transylvanian schoolmates used the traditional bats) until my swan died; then I took the ancient streetcar, which, like the Victorian streetlights, was said to be "the oldest in Europe." This venerable tram groaned its way up the hills so slowly we jumped on its back and rode gratis. Now and then an old conductor, the oldest in Europe, dressed in a threadbare uniform that predated the Hapsburgs, would attempt to shoo away the cluster of children perched on the back of his ancient tram. It was a futile gesture, as he well knew. Only rain and snow kept us off. And it rained and snowed a lot. All through my childhood it rained and snowed without surcease.

Mostly, I walked. The town was full of ghosts and they liked to walk with me and tell me stories. The lower part of the town, where we lived, was linked to the upper by a drawbridge known as "the liars' bridge." On this bridge, lovers lied to each other, and then died of sorrow. Whenever I crossed it, I was besieged by whispers and agonized laments. One night, while I had been wandering in the rain through the alleys of the upper town like a wet cur, I found that the liars' bridge had been raised, and I couldn't return home. I spent the night inside a dry fountain full of damp autumn leaves in a deserted square. A titan embracing a nymph above me protected me from the rain. I traveled farther that night than I ever did using any means of locomotion. I visited places no rockets ever reached. Our speed-driven *fin-de-siècle* has little to tell a child hidden in a fountain in the rain in one of Europe's oldest cities, flying through time wrapped in his thoughts like a black cloak.

New Orleans

ONLY in the old cities—like New Orleans—built long before cars, do walking humans still feel at home. We moved to New Orleans in 1984, the year Orwell's book came true. One of the reasons it came true is that cars, in combination with TV, have made zombies out of everybody with the exception of people lucky enough to live in a pedestrian city where street life is more interesting than television.

In New Orleans life is a pedestrian. People navigate their streets like fish: the streets are our medium, a fluid and changing spectacle that is also the stuff we breathe in and out. It's a city for watching and being watched, a voyeur-voyee paradise that reaches an apogee at Carnival, when everything that can be shown is made manifest, everything that was hidden is displayed, and one's senses are *ambushed*. At Mardi Gras the city becomes impassable to cars. A swelling humanity moves in and out of itself, full of a mysterious and alive intimacy that the drivers of America never experience. New Orleans at Carnival is seditious, un-American, sabotage incarnate—what General Motors sees in nightmares! The huge motorized floats at the head of Mardi Gras parades are grotesque parodies of cars. They insult cars. They move at a pace slower than that of most people. Masked demons perched on top of them shower the intoxicated mob with doubloons, jewels, cigars, panties, and coconuts. People lean on parked cars, sleep on top of them, use them for planters and ashtrays.

After Carnival, cars retake the streets but sheepishly, cautiously, inelegantly. Pedestrians still own the streets. On hot summer nights, at midnight, the citizens sit on their stoops drinking beer and conversing with car drivers stopped in the middle of the street. These are not really cars but slow-crawling gazebos, portable chaise longues. Everyone complains about how bad New Orleans drivers are. In a strict sense, no doubt, it's true. Everybody's drunk or driving that way. In fact, the law requires new drivers in Louisiana to pass the test drunk. It's the only way to survive. New cars sold here all come equipped with air bags and two sizes of drink holders, a large one for beer and a smaller one for bourbon. Drive-by daiquiri places are placed at the entrance of shopping-mall parking lots. Shoppers drop three bucks in the machine and get four ounces of sweetened alcohol to help them shop. Consequently, driving here is a nightmare for orderly people from the rest of America. There are hundreds of casualties when snowbirds from the East come through here in the winter on their way to the Gulf.

Our cemeteries are great, and so are the cafés. Sometimes you can't tell which is which. I often take my coffee to the Lafayette cemetery on Prytania Street and read the paper sitting on somebody's gravestone. My friend Jim Haynes, who lives in Paris, said about New Orleans, "It's Paris!" I know what he meant. Cars haven't completely won.

Ade is the owner of my favorite café in New Orleans, Café Brazil. Ade has never let me pay for coffee or drinks for all the years I've been coming to his establishment. There is a Latin bond between us: Romanian sounds almost like Brazilian, a romance language with a lot of soft, warm sounds. Ade and I came to New Orleans at about the same time. But Ade, unlike me, loves cars. Not just any cars. Old, classic cars, beautiful cars that he parks in front of his place. He barely drives them because he lives around the corner. He is particularly proud of his 1963 Lincoln Continental with the suicide doors. John Kennedy drove in a convertible version of this Lincoln when he was killed in Dallas. "In my country," Ade says, "only the President drives this kind of car."

I see what he means. In my fantasies of return to Romania I saw myself riding into Bucharest thronged by adoring mobs in just this kind of car. I think that for us foreigners America is a collection of fantasy images, the biggest of which is this sort of machine. Immigrants don't want to live in the real America: they want to live in the fantasy America of their youth with all their old friends watching. Many of them do, no matter how long they've been here.

Café Brazil, where I hang out. Best place to watch new tattoos in New Orleans. My friend Ade, who owns the joint, never lets me pay for my double espresso.

Fear and Trembling

I ENROLLED in the Safe Driving School on Tulane Avenue, one of the two establishments in the New Orleans Yellow Pages that spelled "driving" right (unless the "Louisiana Diving School" really teaches "diving with all makes of car").

The day before going to school, I did a bit of hair-raising preschool driving in my friend John Clark's dented reddish vehicle. John is an anarchist. He handed me the keys and quoted Robert Creeley: "Drive, he said." He then seated himself fearlessly next to me, unaware that years ago others had made the mistake of overconfidence. John has me pegged as a surrealist, so when I had gone a piece down the street he

Mr. Carney, my driving teacher. He taught me well and scared me good.

said, "Hmmm. Anarchists don't believe in rules and surrealists believe in making them up. We might need a third party to get us through this here stream-of-traffic consciousness." We did get through it—but not before I clipped an object on the right and lost the side mirror. The object I clipped turned out to be a car. John interpreted my right-leaning driving as political. But I knew better. Years of being to the right of the driver made me misjudge. I was still a passenger. We had lunch and didn't speak of it. My fortune cookie at the end of the meal said, "Soon you will be crossing bridge." As if I needed to be told. There are bridges between one moment and the next, between past and present. I was just now poised to take the wheel and plunge onto one of the shakiest, scariest, most wind-battered bridges of my life.

The Safe Driving School was located on the second floor of a rinky-dink building on a heavily trafficked street in a bad part of town. It could have been the setting for a *film noir*.

My driving teacher, Mr. Carney, was a retired Greyhound bus driver, a tall, handsome black man in his sixties. He exuded authority.

I could see that he had allowed no nonsense during the quarter century he had driven the Dawg. He had put pot smokers and beer drinkers right off the bus. He'd disallowed radio playing without earphones, censured disruptive shouting and obscenity, and forbidden sex in the back seats. Order had reigned on his bus. He was a fatherly figure. He reminded me of Stalin, the Stalin of my childhood, who had watched ever so kindly over me from an oversized portrait above the square. I was in good hands, I thought. I did hope, though, that Mr. Carney had acquired his kindly paternal looks through firm charity rather than the mass murder of peasants.

"We guarantee you the basics of safe driving, and a diploma," Mr. Carney told the class. I had two fellow students: a sixteen-year-old black kid named Tony, who looked bored, and Ravassa, a middle-aged Jewish woman from Beirut. Tony said he already knew how to drive, and was only going through the course *pro forma* for a reason he would rather not discuss. Ravassa was made to come here by her husband. They owned a small gift shop in the French Quarter, and the husband had declared that this was America, and in America women drive the kids to school. "My life was much easier in Beirut," Ravassa said. "I didn't drive there." I knew just what she meant. Civil war, terrorists, and bombs are as nothing compared to the banal instrument of carnage we were about to learn how to operate.

My first driving lesson.
Pedestrians are unaware of the
danger.

"Yes, I've gone ahead and done it," I told myself while watching the car crashes in Mr. Carney's overused educational film. "After twenty-five years as that rarissima of avises in America—the pedestrian—I am going to be a driver. I'll drive a car and I'll have an ID to cash checks with."

Mr. Carney said, "Being a good driver is like being a good Christian—you have to practice every day." OK, I'll be a good driver. I will signal before I turn. I will look before I pass. I will stop before the sign.

But I had problems. Mr. Carney said, "Turn right," and I turned left. "Left," and I turned right. Years of surrealism will do that to a man. Mr. Carney said, "Be polite. Don't turn your brights on a guy just because he's turned them on you. That's like Stevie Wonder meeting Ray Charles." He knew whereof he spoke: most drivers in New Orleans are like Stevie Wonder and Ray Charles. They can sing but they don't look where they are going.

But I was afraid of bigger changes than the lights: Thoughts at fifty miles per hour. Rubber dreams, glass words, metal malaise. Hard shell around soft flesh. The man who ate a car. Cadillac Ranch. UFOs. Mustang Sally. Working at the Cadillac plant. The VW that killed friends of mine. Mr. Carney said, "Get good tires. A tire is like a sneaker. You want it to last more than a week." He was right. I wanted my tires to last. I wanted to last. Meanwhile, I kept adjusting my notions of left and right. Slowly. And getting ready to be Everyman. And when I was going to graduate I was going to drive a car across the U.S.A., and send reports from behind the nouveau wheel.

Driving the same streets I had walked was strange. The trees loomed larger, as if they were straining for attention. I couldn't look up to watch the clouds. I couldn't see small things creeping along the ground. There might have been butterflies around here I was missing completely unless they were ending up as powder and ooze on my windshield. Everything I used to watch with detached and fearless curiosity had now become an enemy. Insects were enemies. Animals were enemies. Pedestrians were enemies. In my head, I was still a pedestrian. I was my own enemy. Only things with roots seemed OK—because they just stood there, watching me pass, another fool going nowhere faster than he had the day before.

But I was doing it. Driving on the road instead of in my head. I was out of my mind.

I once wrote a poem:

> *I hate everything*
> *that moves faster than my body*
> *because everything that moves faster than my body*
> *does so by a cheap trick.*

Now I was moving faster than my body. Every cheap trick Detroit knew was going with me.

Looking at the pyramid of letters in Mr. Carney's office for my eye test, I saw:

E for Entity (the Driving Entity I shall become)

F for Face-off (with my driverless past now lying about me like a discarded coat)

P for Past (once more the Past looks reproachfully at me, a traitor of all that moved naturally)

T for Terror (a Terror different from the various terrors of childhood and adolescence)

L for Laugh (they are Laughing at me)

P for Pistol (I'm going to get one for the glove compartment to be like everyone else in New Orleans: very polite. If you are not polite you get shot)

E for Engine (about which I know nothing)

D for the Devil (he made me do it)

C for Carburetor (the liver of the car: don't drink and drive!)

D for Despair (a new Despair!)

That's how I read the letters, but, on the other hand, why not *Elegance, Felicity, Paradise, Tolerance, Longevity, Pleasure, Ebullience, Desire, Clairvoyance,* and *Daring?* These too, were possible, or at least so said the songs of the car with which I'd been feeding my ears for many days: "Road Runner," "The Modern Lover," "Under My Wheels," "Baby, You Can Drive My Car," "I Get Around . . ."

THE day of the test I experienced a curious mixture of panic, regret, and revulsion. I am always seized by panic when I must deal with the police for any reason whatsoever (a Communist hangover). The regret was for my slower, former self now about to vanish forever in that walking past all humans once belonged to. And revulsion because I had to admit to myself that I might, after all, become a grownup now. (Ha! Little did I know that the car, contrary to common belief, is the enemy of adulthood: it's an adolescent machine.)

"Are you mentally fit to drive?"

It was not a question to be taken lightly. I stared overly long at the pretty officer administering this part of the test. I was *not* mentally fit to drive anything. Not a car. Not a bicycle. Not a boat. I was only fit to drive other people crazy. "Yes," I said.

I then donated my organs. I left my heart to the President of the United States. "He needs it," said my examining officer. I left a number of my internal organs to the Sierra Club, particularly my liver, which they could feed to vultures. I then entered the car, put the key in the ignition, unleashed the brakes, and rolled onto the next stage of my life, camera crew in tow.

True, there was some suspicion among the members of the crew that the overly lenient officer who administered the test was playing for the camera because I did rather abysmally. When she said, "Turn left," I pointed with my hand to the direction I guessed was left, and asked her, "You mean, that way?" When she said yes, I turned, but not before forgetting to signal. At the end of the labyrinthine ordeal she pressed my new driver's ID into my hand, an action that prompted Roger to quip: "You can get anything done with a camera crew present. It doesn't even have to be a real crew."

This remark proved prophetic later on when we experienced one astonishing instance after another of people lying down for the camera like narcotized pets. The American psyche has a hypnotic command written close to the surface: When you see a camera, act. People will display their infirmities, betray their loved ones, cry, bark, and grovel before the Almighty Eye without any prompting or reward whatsoever.

The Party

TO celebrate the momentous occasion and her own release from bondage, Alice threw me a party. She gave me a prophetic print she had made many years ago, after having a strange dream. It depicts yours truly behind the wheel of a big American car and bears the legend: "I dreamt that I went/to the Marxist-Leninist bar/In my big Cadillac car."

People arrived with appropriate gifts. My son Tristan gave me a Nun Molesters T-shirt (in case, I suppose, I was stopped by the police in this overwhelmingly Catholic town). He likes these raw-edge rock groups with names that seem to have been thought up at the moment of impact in a car wreck: Social Disease, Dead Kennedys, Nine Inch Nails, Algebra Suicide. . . .

I got fuzzy dice in white and pink to hang from my window. A drink holder (de rigueur in New Orleans). A bag of kitty litter for icy roads. A painted floor mat. An Elvis hat. And plenty of advice: "Keep the shiny side up and the greasy side down," "Keep your beer on the floor at intersections."

Chris Rose handed me a bottle of bourbon, and said: "This is an American driving fetish. You can drive down the road with an open Jim Beam bottle in one hand and a semiautomatic weapon in the other . . . and you still haven't broken the law!"

My friend Gil burnt his driver's license. "I for one protest this action!" He knows me.

And then there was a loud noise and Jayne Mansfield's head zoomed across the floor on a little toy car and headed straight for me. As the guests gasped, Jayne's headless body walked into the room, holding a remote-control device in her hand. The body said, in the voice of my friend Janet Densmore: "I have a splitting headache!"

"I've never seen a better demonstration of the mind/body split," I told Janet, and meant it. My body may have been technically able to drive but my mind screamed, "No!" Of course, our cameraman, Jean de Segonzac, loved this Hollywood entrance—Janet is a film director and writer—and I had the fleeting vision that all of Hollywood's car-maimed greats were with me now. Jayne's decapitated body was only the first in a long line that stretched with bloody grandeur across the history of cinema. And even before that, Isadora Duncan's scarf fluttered somewhere at the beginning of the motorized century.

NOT all artists have been enamored of cars but avant-garde ones certainly have. Our century began with the Futurists' strident declara-

Jayne Mansfield crashes my driving party.

tions of love to the shiny god of speed. The Futurists' leader, Marinetti, took pride in driving as fast as his Nietzschean delusions of "power" would allow. A little later, in the 1920s, the partying luminaries of the Lost Generation would drive to the Bois de Boulogne in Paris at night, arrange their cars in a circle, and have orgies in the grass under the headlights. Not long after, the lights of Paris went dark as thousands of Nazi cars, motorcycles, and tanks rolled over the Roaring Twenties. Now, those were real car lovers, the Nazis. Yes, we once thought that our headlights would replace the stars.

I also remembered stories about Romania's King Carol, who used to drive over peasants on country roads. There weren't many cars then, but each one was a great gift of power. Now everyone's got the power, and where is the glory? Soon everyone will have a pocket nuke—even more power.

The party went on very late and then everyone who could got in their cars and went home.

Next day, I had a Jayne Mansfield-sized headache. I was now as prepared as any American for the rites of driving.

Cars and *the* Car

McILWAIN CADILLAC is one of those All-American dealerships in the heart of Jefferson Parish just outside New Orleans. Jefferson Parish, where car dealerships vie with each other to display the largest American flags possible, was home to David Duke's failed campaign to become America's first Nazi president. Happily, he was erased from the political scene, but at McIlwain's he was undoubtedly still the choice. My blue-jeaned looks did not exactly go with the neon smoothness of the showroom. I was definitely not the Cadillac type, but in a recession you can't afford to be a snob. Mr. Dan Jones, the jolly salesman who showed me the new Cadillacs, was cordial. "What sort of Caddy are we looking for?" he asked me, using the plural as if he and I were part of that infinitesimal tasteful minority of Cadillac people. "An expensive one," I said. "I just came to America and I want to pay as much as possible." That's just what he liked to hear.

"Welcome to America," he said. Thank you. I sprawled on the beige leather interior of a mammoth model and closed my eyes. "How does it feel?" he asked. "Like sleep," I said.

I didn't like the new cars. The interiors were like sleep. They reminded me of the plush insides of coffins. And the exteriors looked like new Burger Kings. "Where are the fins?" I asked Mr. Jones. "Those are long gone," he said, momentarily nostalgic. "Those were gone by the mid-sixties."

That was just about when I got here. I must have witnessed in fact the exact historical moment when the last abbreviated nubs of these Caddy's once mighty fins left the planet and vanished. By the time I got here, in 1966, things weren't going so well. Half of my generation had gotten inside tiny German cars and driven West, leaving their parents' Caddies in their suburban garages, along with the golf carts and the dreams of corporate order. The other half left their cars in garages, their adolescence in parking lots, their weeping parents in their kitchens, their girlfriends at train stations, and were shipped off to Vietnam. By the end of the sixties, the cars themselves had lost all their confidence. They lost their fins, their chrome—they lost weight, and—ultimately—they lost their shape. These new Caddies looked like square lumps of self-conscious matter, not sure if they were meant to move or to melt. Gas wasn't cheap anymore.

Whenever they make lists of people Americans trust the least, car salesmen show up right near the top. I don't know. Mr. Dan Jones seemed like a decent enough chap to me. He seemed grandfatherly and weary like any middle-class overweight southern white American who couldn't understand what the hell happened to this country since my generation took to the roads. But he didn't have to go very far to understand. The truth was staring him in the face; he was surrounded by the truth. The truth was rolling off the truck as we spoke. The truth was the new Cadillacs, all of them made with cheap plastic, looking unassuming, ungainly, formless, and lumpy like cold mashed potatoes. The America he was selling went to pot because he was selling a cheap, plastic, planned-for-obsolescence product made carelessly for the sole purpose of selling more and more of it. The Cadillacs of the past were like the Americans of the past: cocky, self-assured, naïve, naturally bigoted, and optimistic. Eisenhower Americans with fins and classic bodies. It wasn't my generation that ruined America. It was America that ruined America. Mr. Dan Jones ruined America. But he was (is) a nice guy. And he probably voted for David Duke.

America isn't what it used to be. David Duke doesn't drive a Cadillac; he drives a VW. He didn't go to Vietnam, but he didn't go West with the hippies either. He stayed right here in Louisiana and dressed in a Nazi uniform, and worked his way up to Grand Wizard of the KKK. And he almost won a seat in the United States Senate with the help of new Caddy owners.

"I think I'll go find an old car," I told the disappointed salesman. "Did you vote for David Duke?" "That's my business, now, isn't it?" he answered tartly. "Don't get me wrong," I said, "but get Duke to change cars. VWs are un-American." He agreed with that. And shrugged wearily.

America in the last decade of the millennium is a complicated place. Our shoes come from Italy. Our cars come from Japan. Our patriots come from Nazi Germany. Immigrants are buying Caddies. Romanians teach English to Americans. And the money is shit. You could buy a house twenty years ago for what it costs to buy a Caddy now.

Only a few days before, while I was still a pedestrian, I'd gone to a rally against David Duke in New Orleans. Marching is one of the last pedestrian pleasures left. People don't march much in America anymore; they aren't walking a whole lot either. A rally in the sixties would bring out thousands, tens of thousands, even hundreds of thousands of people. This was pathetic! A few hundred of us went shouting slogans past cemeteries. Now *there* were some voters that needed persuading. The angels on gravestones looked interested but they don't vote.

Most of the American electorate votes like the dead these days. Maybe it's because everybody drives alone inside his or her bubble instead of walking, marching, and shouting. Every car in America ought to have a tombstonelike sign on it: HERE LIES A VOTER. Drive on, citizens!

On the Moonwalk by the Mississippi

THAT evening, after McIlwain, I went to the Mississippi River at sunset and sat on a rock. The sounds of my old city were all around me. A calliope, giving off puffs of steam. A drunk singing. The clink of silverware in the cafés of the French Quarter. The soft chatter of people seated on the Spanish balconies. The hooves of horses clattering on cobblestones. I love horses.

Horses are cars you can eat if you're hungry.

Something was happening to me. The winter of my discontent. Middle Age? Boredom? The thought that I might be missing something? It was too late to be a teenager experiencing the backseat of my first car. Too late to listen to my car radio in the early sixties. Too late to be a kid in a big, bad car. Still not too late, perhaps, to send back to Romania pictures of myself at the wheel. A tug went by on the river,

I look over the Mississippi River, remembering Mark Twain whose complete works I read in Romanian when I was ten years old. The great American river has become Cloaca Maxima, *the great American sewer. "Every glass of water in New Orleans," a café wit once told me, "has been drunk six times."*

pushing barges full of coal. There was only one man in the engine room, reading by a lamp. I wanted to be him. The tug sighed mournfully as the last drops of sun sank into the river and everything turned violet. It was the twilight of the century.

Was it too late to discover America, which seems to get discovered over and over and never definitively? How much did I really know about my new country if I never got off the highway in places the streetcar, the bus, or the train didn't go?

Cars of Yesteryear

NOT far from McIlwain, there is a modest garage entrance in a square white building. It's a quiet street with little to distinguish it. But once the garage door swings open, you enter a fabulous world of vintage automobiles. This is Cars of Yesteryear, a private collection of fine cars for rent and for sale. Here they are, Packards, Checkers, Fords, luxury cars, muscle cars, space cars. I admire their polished fenders, their outrageous fins, the fantasies they embody. These cars come charged with lore from the past, after having taken a detour through the movies.

This is like walking into an idealized dream of America. I look around for broad-shouldered, smiling squares with "I Like Ike" buttons. And prom queens stepping into the cars, helped by their boyish dates—ready to zoom into a bright, futuristic future of automated kitchens and perfect lawns. The space age has begun, America is rich, the Russians are definitely the bad guys, things are pretty much black and white. Well, they are mostly white really. The civil rights movement is only a blip on the screen. Vietnam not even that. It's hard to believe that everyone in America used to drive these elongated beauties. It is strange also to see them here, classics now, in a museum of sorts. Yesterday's everydayness has become classical so fast. It's a sleight of hand, a kind of collapsed-time magic. After all, 1960 wasn't so long ago—or was it? Is it possible that everything we *now* take for granted is already creeping into a museum? That nostalgia's eating at my objects even as I speak? Even the car my father drove is somewhere hereabouts. . . . There it is! That *is* the car my father drove!

I'd love to see America from one of these babies. It would be like taking an old mirror with the reflection of another time frozen in it and holding it up to the present. If I drove one of McIlwain's new

The car my father drove, minus my father.

dilly-bobs I'd feel like I was going shopping—instead of venturing into
a mystery.

These old cars are a lot like the America I imagined before I came
here—a country still being made, where distance and strangeness are
no match for youth and desire. Long, powerful, brash, shiny, slick, fast
. . . the shrewd, adventurous, and cruel America of Al Capone, Henry
Miller's air-conditioned nightmare, the heartbreaking road of Jack
Kerouac, the psychotic badlands of Charlie Starkweather (with Cybill

Shepherd), Allen Ginsberg's Wichita vortex sutra on Bob Dylan's tape-recorder . . .

The old cars gave off an exuberant giddiness, a musk of eternal youth, a Huck Finn feeling off their shiny huck fins. They said, "You're an American, you can start over again, the mystery of America has barely been touched."

Of course, most Americans got in their big spaceship cars and headed mostly to their suburban planets—abandoning the old cities and leaving mountains of garbage behind. Still, they gave off the feeling—which is also the secret birthright of every American—that if things didn't work out where you lived you could always get in your car and go someplace else. The future they escaped into didn't turn out to be so rosy after all. Still, these were the jalopies of eternal youth, and I touched them tenderly, running my hand over their mirrored surfaces. Their drivers got old fast; the cars didn't.

Andrei Got His Car

I GOT a red '68 Cadillac convertible.

I wanted a '66—for the year I came, and for the route famous in songs—but I settled for a '68. That was the year of the Chicago Democratic Convention, the Paris uprising, the riots following the assassination of Martin Luther King. In 1968 I was in Detroit, Michigan, living amid the ruins of the inner city burnt to the ground in 1967.

In 1968, José Feliciano sang, "C'mon, baby, light my fire!" from every FM dial in every car in America. And outside, you could hear them shouting, "Burn, baby, burn!" It was the hot summer of 1968, the Summer of Hate that followed the Summer of Love of 1967.

At the end of 1968, I moved to the Lower East Side of New York.

New York

America is a vast place, and I doubt that any man knows it thoroughly. It's possible too to live in a place and not know anything about it, because you don't want to know.

Henry Miller, *The Air-Conditioned Nightmare*

I LIKE cities that start with "New": New York, New Orleans, New Rochelle, New Haven . . . there are hundreds of them in the New World. Every one of them was set up to be the New Jerusalem, the place where the sins of the old were cleansed, without losing the amenities of their origins. I thought that it might be interesting to visit the myriad of "new" cities in order to see what, if anything, they still had in common with those origins. I already knew the ironic answers, of course.

New York, for instance, which used to be New Amsterdam, was once ruled by the Dutch governor Peter Stuyvesant, who complained to his queen that there were entirely "too many Jews" in the city. Stuyvesant is now buried across the street from the best—for my money—Jewish deli in New York, the (what else) Second Avenue Deli, on Second Avenue. This neighborhood was the heart of Jewish life in America. The queen didn't reply to Stuyvesant's panicked dispatch, but her descendant, another Dutch queen, came to pay her respects at his grave in the late 1960s. The crowd watched the monarch, clad in a simple dress with a huge hat on her head, descend from her limousine. A disappointed child behind me said, "I've seen a lot better queens!" He was right. I'd seen a lot better queens, too. In fact, some of them were right in the crowd. *Jewish* queens, too.

27

The new cities of America really are new. Only New York, of all of them, still retains some of its subterranean links to Europe, though it has radically altered them. "Ah, New York!" a snobbish Frenchman once told me. "New York is only Europe with an *erection!* New *Mexico*, now that's America!"

In my opinion, New York is less European than New Mexico is Mexican, but who wants to argue with a Frenchman? Since Alexis de Tocqueville the French have always thought they know more about America than Americans.

I wanted to start my car trip in New York because it is where I first landed in 1966. New York was the very beginning.

I resolved to take my Caddy (a car named after the chief of a tribe of native American pedestrians) from New York to California, a west-ward journey I made once before, at the end of the sixties, together with thousands of my generation. We migrated in a big wave from the cities of the Midwest and the East to California, where the Promised Land had moved.

Alice and I left New York in 1970 after meeting a German guy named Erhard in front of the Gem Spa on Second Avenue. Erhard and his girlfriend Glenda had obtained a car from an agency that paid people to drive cars for executives moving to California. It didn't take long for us to make up either our minds or our bundles of clothes, books, manuscripts, and drawings. We floated out of New York as lightly as if we were wind-borne spores. We left behind the tough streets with their patina of irony and murder, and plunged into the West, joining countless station wagons full of children who had the same idea simultaneously. California, true to its reputation, was gentle on our souls, and not particularly fond of the strictures of reality. Time passed there the way it passes in a fairy tale: one day was ten years, ten years were but the blink of an eye. One morning I woke up and saw my face emerge from the mirror. I remembered New York.

We returned East, to an oddly real world, where people got up in the morning and went to work. I had forgotten all about rush hour, the tired faces behind newspapers on subways filled with psychotic ima-ginings, the throbbing restaurants, the cologne of ambition, the high tides of neon. . . . This was a dream, too, but one in which everyone took speed to stay awake.

IT'S later still now, as I grip the wheel of my dream-mobile stuck in downtown Broadway traffic. Another ten years have passed, and I'm waking up in Dream No. 3, looking once more at my face. Only this time I'm looking in the rearview mirror. Not for long, though. Two bums with rags have launched themselves like street rockets onto my windshield, marring its perfection with oily streaks, and I start to scream. It's a primal scream. A driver is born.

I WANT to go back to places where I once lived carlessly and drive through my own dreamy past, perhaps *over* my own dreamy past—or whatever is left of it in a country that loves to erase its past as fast as it builds the future.

How do people live now? I wondered.

I FIRST saw New York in my third-grade Communist schoolbook. "Look at the ugly buildings where the capitalists live!" said the caption. I thought they looked grand. I was very small. The book should have said, "Look at the grand buildings the ugly capitalists live in!"

The Nuyorican Café

WHEN the traffic moved, I shot past the bums and drove to the Nuyorican Café, not far from where I used to live, on the Lower East Side of Manhattan. I parked my shiny convertible in front of the place I used to live. A crowd of nostalgic old folk and admiring young hoods gathered to admire my jalopy. I jumped over the side, as I had seen Elvis and Chris Rose do, and picked my dignified self from the sidewalk when my savoir-faire and my aim failed to coincide.

The Nuyorican is where New York Spanish-speaking poets invented a whole new poetry language (newyorican), and where performance, rap, and street sound come to find an audience. My friend Bob Holman, the famous "Plain White Rapper," also known as Panic DJ, emcees at The Nuyorican.

PRE-TRIP RAP AT THE NUYORICAN BEFORE A HOT CROWD OF (MOSTLY) COOL HIPSTERS, MY FRIEND PHILIP HERTER, AND THE (UBIQUITOUS) CAMERA

The road is a metaphor factory. It spews poetry, songs, maxims, homilies, quips, stupidities, and profundities. Everyone knows that life is a journey and time is a road. Everyone knows that. Babies, who travel a piece to get here, know that. They journey into the world via the meta-road. They wear sunglasses and drive tiny cars made out of light beams. Life is a road and a cliché factory. It's the source of practically everything we humans try to tell ourselves about ourselves. You look like a mile of bad road. You've taken the road less traveled.

I haven't driven very far yet.

The road is everything except for one thing—real. You can say everything you want about the road, and you do. You might even live your life using road metaphors every day to get you to work and back, but the sad fact is there is no road. The last time there was road was in the sixties. We had road back then because Neal Cassady liked to drive, Jack Kerouac liked to write, and everyone wanted to leave home. So all at once for about ten years young people discovered the infrastructure at the very same moment that they saw their own arteries and veins with the blood rushing through them all lit up. The infrastructure all neon-lit and gas-station-neoned throbbed briefly with all these young Americans with lit veins and arteries rushing along its highways and byways. These lit infusions were driven along by sounds they themselves made singing of the roads they rode on.

And when they stopped moving, sometime in the late seventies, there was this big store of road lore floating in the psycho-sphere. It's where the Reagan-Bush decades went shopping for images to get people off the road and into schools, homes, corner offices, prisons, and mental institutions. Which is where we all live now.

Roads aren't real anymore. All roads are now metaphors about the road. Most people would rather stay home. In their homes they feed on lots of clichés about the road so that they won't feel as if they've stopped moving. Only the dead stop moving and most people don't want to be dead. Every couch potato dreams himself or herself on the road, and they are, thanks to TV, which gives them the illusion that they are somewhere else. Everyone lives on TV now, which is everywhere and nowhere. People are in the Amazon, in the Arctic, on the streets of Detroit, in the

Southwest, in San Francisco all at once, by remote control. When TV travelers do travel they go to places they've seen on TV, straight into the tourist postcards and never see what they haven't already seen at home. If they stumble on something that's never been on TV they shoot it with the video camera and then it's on TV. They go from postcard to postcard by plane so they never touch the road. Cars aren't big and strong enough to go a serious distance anymore. They are all made out of collapsible plastic with these dinky engines and they are—safe. They reek of safety and go practically nowhere. Everybody's safe and going nowhere. That's how it is now. Nothing you can do about it. Or almost nothing.

I'm gonna go in my big car down the roads of my past, which is also the past when people were on the road. I'm gonna give rides to hitchhiking ghosts. I'm gonna go to the car factory to see who took the road out of the car. I'm gonna go to where cars killed my friends in California on a curvy road. I'm gonna drive to the past. "The past," as J. B. Priestley said, "is a foreign country. They do things differently there." They sure do. Did. Still doing. I've been on a lot of airplanes and felt nothing. Except reconstituted—like astronaut food.

The Statue of Liberty

I CRIED when I first saw her. The two hundred salami-chomping Yugoslavs aboard the jet bringing us to the New World saw her too, and broke into a Serbian rendition of "America the Beautiful." We were done with the old world, liberty was ours! We emerged like butterflies from the husks of abandoned salamis onto the tarmacs of the Promised Land.

On the ferry going to Liberty Island, I asked a number of people—mostly foreign tourists or recent immigrants—why they were going to visit her. A Portuguese man said that he had lived under the dictatorship of Salazar and the statue had always represented democracy to him. A Chinese woman said that she had been in Tiananmen Square when the students had erected a Chinese Miss Liberty. An Italian man said that he just wanted to get a picture. But it was a middle-aged man with a German accent who said the simplest and most moving thing:

"I came to this country in 1939." That's all. He then looked me straight in the eye.

I could only barely imagine how Miss Liberty must have looked to a European Jew fleeing the Nazis in 1939.

I have seen her in movies, in books, in cartoons, in commercials, on postcards, on T-shirts, tattooed on a guy's arm. I've heard her spoken of lyrically, bitterly, and wistfully in poems, songs, newspapers. An overwrought familiar, equally a torch of idealism and a mistress of kitsch!

I SAW her a few years back, encased in scaffolding, the object of a major renovation spearheaded by Lee Iacocca, the Chrysler executive. She looked to me like Reagan's America imprisoned in new conservative restraints. I told this to Ken Burns, who was making a movie about her, and I emphasized my point by pointing up and saying: "Raise your arm if you're sure!" It occurs to me now that several ironies met then: a car executive restoring our liberties, a Romanian immigrant quoting a television commercial, a filmmaker marking the moment. . . .

MARK, LIBERTY PARK RANGER

AC: *Is there some sort of device that keeps birds and things off of the flame?*

RANGER MARK: *Absolutely not. No device at all.*

AC: *The biggest statue I ever saw was in my hometown. It was a statue of Stalin. It was massive, it was not big like Miss Liberty. He had his feet planted firmly in the ground. And his head was equipped with some kind of pigeon-killing ray and the pigeons fell down and there was a whole population that lived off the meat at his feet.*

RANGER MARK: *Oh my goodness.*

No tourists came to see Stalin. You certainly couldn't climb up inside him, but the Russian writer Vladimir Maximov says that an old man raised goats in a metal cave inside his boot. There was also a mountain in front of my house with the name S T A L I N spelled with trees. After 1963 they let trees grow in the hollows of his name and he slowly

Ranger Mark and I shake on the deal. I can take the statue home.

vanished. The L alone took my whole thirteenth year to disappear.

There are tourists from dozens of countries at Miss Liberty's feet. Every nationality has a different group arrangement for picture taking. Eastern Europeans pose women in front with men behind. The Japanese like rows by height, with children crouching in front. Israelis link arms.

My mother was a photographer. She snapped groups throughout my childhood. There are tourists in my nightmares. That's how I know that they are nightmares. Tourists are terrorists with cameras. Terrorists are tourists with guns.

I admire Ms. Liberty's stoic patience—always in the eternal flashbulb, the perennial cover girl of democracy. How does she keep her soul camera-proof as we turn her into postcards?

THE GLOBE

SHORTLY before the end of the Soviet Union and the reshuffling of all the borders of Europe, an old Jew asked a Soviet border guard for a globe to see where he should go. After studying it for a few hours, he returned it and asked: "Do you have another globe?"

The Global Thinker.

Dash Needs

I NEED something for the dash of my car. How about this snow-glow thing? You shake it and it snows under her. I asked the Nigerian guy who owned the stand if he had one where it snows on top of her. Nope. He had Liberty belt buckles, watches, scarves, shorts, bathing suits, and Boy Scout knives. But that was it for snow.

He was from Nigeria and it doesn't snow there—either under or on top of things.

(It did snow in 1965 in Italy, a rare occurrence, to be sure, and not an entirely pleasant surprise to my mother and me, who were in transit to America then, and living in an unheated room. My friend Julian and I went looking for something to sell to someone so we could buy some wood. Failing that, we would have liked to get enough cash to stay all day in a café. We had but 100 lire between us, which wasn't even enough for an espresso. We watched a couple of ancient winos roll cigarettes from discarded butts but this was obviously a highly skilled occupation. We dove off a bridge into the freezing cold water of Naples Bay in the snow, in the vain hope that the rich American tourists wandering up above would throw us a few coins. We were quite prepared to dive for them. Naturally, they averted their gazes from our shivering, goosebumpy selves. We did bum some sticks of gum off a sailor but found its resale value to be nil. In the end, we kept ourselves warm with fantasies of America. We'll come back! We'll show the bastards!)

ON the other hand, I might be better off with a watch. You need to know all the time what time it is in America. It's getting worse all the time, too. Time's gotten a hundred times faster since I came here and it was already a thousand times faster than time in Romania.

Semilegal and illegal aliens stand right outside the Statue of Liberty's ferry dock and sell good imitation Rolexes and Swatches. Foreign tourists fresh off the tour boat gobble them up. They keep time just like the real thing. Actually, they keep time *better* than the real thing because you can wear the fakes anywhere in any weather at any time. Real Rolexes you have to leave at home when you come to certain places like this park where they sell fakes.

I fell for the watch scam in Italy. My mother and I had fifty dollars to our name. It was supposed to last for six months. Coming home late from vagabonding through the back alleys of Naples, I met a dapper young guy who showed me several gold watches in a nice leather case. He explained that he was an employee of the airport and that he had stolen these Swiss gold watches the day before but hadn't been able to sell them. Now he had to go back to work and he needed to sacrifice them for only $200 each. After some pretty shrewd bargaining on my part, I got him down to two watches for $50. He waited outside the building for me while I rushed into our little room and took our life savings out of the little drawer by my mother's bed. She didn't wake up. In the morning, when she did, she saw two gold watches lying beautifully opulent on top of the little table. "Look what I did with our fortune!" I exclaimed proudly. My mother examined them anxiously, noting the 24-karat-gold stamp and their satisfying weight. Shortly before noon that day they stopped ticking. We opened them up and in there, instead of complex jewel mechanisms, were the two rusty steel springs that had kept their hearts temporarily beating.

Welcome to the West! We didn't eat anything for the next couple of weeks.

Ellis Island

IT was never easy to get into the Promised Land. It certainly was no picnic for me. Half of all Americans living today have someone who came through Ellis Island. They waited here to find out if they would be held, deported, or let in. They washed over the island in waves, millions and millions of them, all of them done with the Old World, ready to be reborn. Steins ready to become Stones, Rosens Rosses, Cardarellis Ca ds, Witkevieczes Vicks, Codrescus Corkscrews.

Immigration officers walked glumly among them, looking for anarchists like Emma Goldman and poets like me to send back. I fought them for ten years to get my citizenship. They thought I was a Communist poet spy. But that was progress: in Romania just "poet" was enough to get you noticed by the police.

I spoke with Ranger Peter in "the room of the final judgment."

AC: *We are now in the room of the final judgment and that's enough to give me a shiver. My fear of these things has to do with the fact that it took me so long to get my citizenship. You see, I think they thought I was an anarchist, but that was their idea.*

RANGER PETER: *That's possible, I don't know. You know, I don't know your case, why they would think that. You don't look like one to me.*

So many of us, so much hunger! So much flag waving! Eyes looking out on promises and deceptions. Gotta keep your eyes open for *trompe l'oeil!*

Sammy's Roumanian Restaurant

THEY are celebrating either the collapse of Communism or the Fall of Rome here at Sammy's Roumanian Restaurant.

Some of us came to America to be free. Most of us came here to eat. Here, being a vegetarian—which I happen to be—is probably dangerous. Everyone eats as if they'd just escaped from the gulag.

Some have. Ion is a yoga teacher hounded for years by Ceauşescu's secret police. Another waited ten years to join her beloved in America. They and I made it. We all know someone who didn't. One of my classmates suffocated in the smokestack of a ship leaving Constantsa. Another was shot by a border guard. The police mind is the same everywhere. But here we can relax a little—over stacks of potato pancakes, enormous mounds of stuffed cabbage, mountains of pickles, boiled tongue longer than the plate it comes on, jam and sweet cheese with dill rolled in thin pancakes, glass bowls of fried chicken livers. There are also containers of chicken fat—schmaltz—on every table to pour on top of meat already fried in chicken fat. Sammy's uses salt, fat, and sugar with kamikaze liberality.

ION: *In Romania there was no meat, so I can't believe this is meat.*

WAITER: *Veal chops . . . Potato pancakes . . .*

ION: *If they gonna see this in Romania they're going to kill us, you know?*

SAMMY: *He's not going back to Romania, he's staying in New York! This is the way everybody eats in New York! This is the way every-*

*At Sammy's Roumanian Restaurant in New York with
Romanian refugees.*

*body eats in New York every day. There's the steak! Anybody don't
know the words, just move your lips!*

A creature like Sammy can exist only in New York. Short, loud,
self-engendered, a dozen gold chains around his neck, babbling gibber-
ish in a dozen languages, he is like a golem of schmaltz, born from the
trampled mud of Eastern Europe, the muck at the bottom of immigrant boats. He proclaims his well-being at the top of his lungs. His
laughter is nothing short of insane, a kind of anguished cry that must
sound like a grotesque parody of triumph to his diners, some of whom
still have numbers tattooed on their arms.

Faded torch singers bellow, sweaty violinists torture their strings in
your ears . . . we are in prewar Austria-Hungary . . . decadence . . . top
hats floating on a river of paprikash . . . it's a howl raised against a
world that cut short these people's youth. Outside, in the guarded
parking lot (it's a bad neighborhood) there are limos, Rollses, Mer-
cedeses . . . all the desperate wealth of people with a big hole inside
that can't be filled no matter how much schmaltz you pour into it.

Haitians

AROUND the corner from Sammy's there is another hole in the wall. Not all political refugees were created equal. There are twenty Haitians squatting in this abandoned building on the Lower East Side. They are intelligent, streetwise cats, who present themselves as an extended family, a "squat," a certain alternative form of living. True, it's a crack-smoking family, addicted and poor, but a family nonetheless, with its own lore and habits and hopes.

They speak four languages, French, Patois, English, and Oogoo-Boogoo. I ask them what that is, and they tell me that it's what they speak in America when they don't want the "man" to know what they are saying. They laugh every time they say "Oogoo-Boogoo."

I ask them if they cook in there. "No, we order out," says one of my friends. "Chinese."

AC: *Do they deliver?*

HAITIAN 1: *They don't come in here to deliver.*

AC: *When you came to America, what did you think?*

HAITIAN 2: *America is one of the most wonderful places. There is food, money, jobs, you know . . .*

HAITIAN 1: *America, it's like you come here and pick the money off the trees. You know, the money dropping down—you get everything in America which is a definite surprise.*

HAITIAN 1 TO AC: *What's the best thing and the worst thing for you, I mean, here?*

AC: *For me, it was that I could come here and talk about anything. Because in my country if I talked or wrote about certain things I could go to prison for it. The worst thing is I can't always get people to pay attention.*

HAITIAN 3: *Same thing in my country too.*

Haitian squatters on the Lower East Side in New York. We
are waiting for a raid by the Housing Authority.

HAITIAN 2: *You got certain more freedom in this place that you don't*
have nowhere else.

HAITIAN 1: *This is why this is . . . America.*

They also tell me that in America you can go to sleep a poor man
and wake up a millionaire. Meanwhile, they may wake up without
their home. Across the street, officials from the New York Housing
Authority wait for us to leave so that they can evict them. When I point
out the fat guys with toothpicks waiting for our cameras to disappear,
the Haitians set up a righteous howl of indignation. They point to
another abandoned building across the street. "That's a squat, too! But
they are white! They want us out because we are black! Racism." I
don't doubt it. We hang around with our camera (Roger's film-crew

notion proven right once more!) but eventually we have to go. Two days later, we go back to see what happened. The entrance to the squat has been cemented. There is no one around.

An Urban Pioneer

HERE on the Lower East Side, amid the refuse of generations of poor immigrants and bohemian refugees from America, I find a new urban pioneer who has staked out a postage-stamp garden. It's a middle-aged black woman with a kindly smile. I asked her if life was hard around here. "For plants it's easy," she said. "They get lots of love. For humans, that's different."

HUMANS have been dying here. AIDS has taken a devastating toll among the young denizens of the art ghetto. The homeless have been routed from Tompkins Square Park. Every morning many of them do not wake up.

It was pretty bad when I lived here in the late sixties. There were homeless then, too, and drugs took people now and then. There were police harassment and community action. There was the neighborhood defense group called The Motherfuckers. And The Pagans motorcycle club. And, of course, it was a lot of fun too: apartments were cheap, drugs were plentiful and interesting, all one's friends were young and full of poetry, and there was a certain camaraderie on the streets. All of that past seems innocent now, like Eden, compared to the massive destruction of the nineties. On the other hand, there are new art galleries, fancy boutiques, chic little restaurants, nightclubs, gourmet shops. Hell has gotten worse but heaven, too, has gotten more heavenly.

Allen Ginsberg

ALLEN GINSBERG, the father of three generations of American rebels, has lived on the Lower East Side since his youth. He is the king of this capital of bohemia that shelters the poet and artist refugees from the American dream, as well as the literal refugees who are looking for it. I came to present my credentials to Allen as soon as I arrived here in 1966. I looked him up on Tenth Street, an address given to me in the strictest confidence by an Italian poet. A Puerto Rican family was taking the pale March sun on the front steps of his tenement building. "Does Allen Ginsberg live here?" I asked, sure of the resounding renown of the great poet. They consulted for a length of time, then said: "We don't know who that is." I stepped into the dark hallway and studied the mailboxes pried open with teenage screwdrivers. "Ginsberg/Orlovsky," one of them said. I knocked loudly on the door.

A rail-thin skinny, dripping-wet naked man opened the door. It was Peter Orlovsky. Allen wasn't home, and Peter did not speak since he was spending all his time in the bathtub in silent meditation. I waited for a few minutes and was ready to bolt when Allen came home. He made tea, spoke to me cordially in French, gave me books of poetry, smiled a lot, and made me feel most welcome. Allen's legendary kindness took in the runty Romanian of 1966 without any reservation. How different and how kind were the poets compared to the brutish Immigration types who looked at me as if I were some species of lice. . . .

Now I wanted Allen's blessing for this trip into nineties America. I got the blessing over blintzes at the Odessa Ukrainian Restaurant, with a story. Allen told me that a month or so before he had brought Bob Dylan to Tompkins Square Park across the street, hoping to interest him in the plight of the homeless who were about to be evicted by the police. Allen, who is never without his camera, was simultaneously

OPPOSITE. *Lower East Side, New York. A memorial to a local activist. His birthday is the same as mine, December 20. I am twenty-three years older.*

Allen Ginsberg and I at St. Mark's Church in New York,
discussing ways to remove Peter Stuyvesant from the
graveyard to bury Ted Berrigan there instead.

attempting to snap the scene for posterity. Dylan, who always fears
being recognized, and hates to be photographed besides, was very
nervous about Allen's taking his picture. The homeless, suspicious of
Dylan's nervousness, thought that the two were cops. They surrounded
them and started shouting and throwing bottles at them. And so it
came to pass that two of America's greatest bards, a poet and a singer,
were ignominiously chased out by the very people they were discussing
helping. Photography and fidgeting are a bad combination.

IN the fifties, Allen's friend Jack Kerouac left from here to go On the
Road. A whole generation followed him. I asked Allen about Kerouac's
America. Allen told me that America in the nineties is very much like

Kerouac's America in the fifties, only more so: more pollution, more waste, more holes in the atmosphere, more conformity, more despair, more ignorance.

"The Land is an Indian thing," Kerouac said, and Allen repeated it, significantly. I knew it, too, from many years ago. But is it still an Indian thing?

Manhattan used to be an Indian thing. The Indians sold it to the Dutch for $24 and have been getting screwed ever since.

Kerouac and I have something else in common. I can barely drive, and neither could he. Eddie Kerouac, his first wife, told me that Jack knew only how to back up, which Neal Cassady taught him after getting him a job parking cars. But Neal was a great driver, and I have no Neal. What I have instead is a camera crew. Visiting your past with a camera crew is like taking witnesses to the sites of long-ago crimes. There may be nothing there but the witnesses' faith. On the other hand, what was there to begin with?

Scott, our soundman, visited Kerouac's grave in Lowell, Massachusetts, and this is what he saw: one bottle of cheap red wine with a note around its neck, "To Jack, from Henri"; a can of Chock Full O' Nuts; a coffee can full of pennies; a Chevy hubcap with rainwater in it; and the last page from a paperback copy of *On the Road*. America.

After lunch, Allen and I walked to St. Mark's Church in the Bowery, a place of poetry readings and youth crimes. Buried here in the front yard is Peter Stuyvesant, Dutch governor of New Amsterdam, notorious anti-Semite. I quoted Stuyvesant's famous letter to the queen about the Jews. Allen didn't know this about Stuyvesant, whose familiar name hangs on everything from bridges to neighborhoods. I proposed taking Stuyvesant out of there and burying Ted Berrigan in his stead. Ted, a great poet and a legendary man of the Lower East Side, had been the *deus ex machina* of St. Mark's Church, and like Allen, inspirer of a whole generation of poets. Ted Berrigan wrote:

> *People of the Future*
> *while you are reading these poems, remember*
> *you didn't write them,*
> *I did.*

Ted died on July 4, 1983. He had already written several epitaphs for himself, including: "Nice to see you!" He certainly deserved a place in the cemetery at St. Mark's: he was an includer of people, a true American, not an excluder like Stuyvesant. Allen agreed to the plan. We are going to get a hundred thousand signatures to put Berrigan in Stuyvesant's place.

Walt Whitman

DRIVING at twilight out of New York, I could feel the impatience of my car. It strains at the bit and it grows longer, stretching like a sleek cat as the lights of Manhattan fade behind me.

Where are we going, Walt Whitman?
Which way does your beard point tonight?

That's what Allen Ginsberg asked the old graybeard poet, father of American poetry, whose bold heartbeat still draws us on. Where is Whitman's America in the uncertain, fearful, angry xenophobic nineties? Has Whitman become merely the name of a highway stop for gas and cigarettes?

Whitman designed his own grave near Camden, New Jersey, and paid more for it than he did for his house. Our most optimistic poet had no fear of the future. He planned to have visitors after his death.

While I was visiting his grave, the gatekeeper of the cemetery came to hand me a fax. It said, "Hotel reservation confirmed in Chicago." That was nice. Now I had a place to sleep, too. Whitman, who was enamored of the telegraph, would have liked, I think, the swiftness of our world, which can reach even a man standing quietly by a grave. He would not have liked—as I didn't—the rudeness of the interruption. I would have preferred to communicate with Whitman himself by psychic fax. Maybe I was—the place was throbbing with messages.

At the entrance to the cemetery there were two signs. Their arrows pointed in different directions. One of them said: WHITMAN'S TOMB. The other: NICK VIRGILIO'S GRAVE. "Who's Nick Virgilio?" I asked the gatekeeper. "Another poet," he said. "So many people came asking for him we put up a sign. He was from Camden, too. He wrote haiku, I think."

Walt Whitman's grave, throbbing with messages. Whitman's brother, who never responded to the poet's anguished pleas for money, is also buried here for some reason.

I think I could turn and live with animals [Whitman wrote], *they're so placid and self-contain'd.*

And so are the dead. I once visited a great collector of Whitman first editions in Detroit, who did not let me touch any of the books. "But Whitman," I exclaimed, "he wanted to be with the reader in the open air, he begged his readers to touch him!" "That may be," the collector replied, "but what can he do about it now?"

Whitman's Children

WHITMAN lived in Camden, New Jersey, with a man and a woman, sexually manifold and optimistic, the spokesman of liberty in all its guises. Urban renewal, whatever that is, has rolled over this neighborhood, leaving only Walt's home, though there is something new across the street—a prison.

I walked over to talk to the young women who were making mysterious hand gestures to their men behind bars.

AC: *Hi, who do you have in there?*

WOMAN: *My uncle Mike and my boyfriend Ed.*

AC: *How did you develop this language?*

WOMAN: *Well, I learned it like four years ago, and it's only writing out the letters with your hands.*

AC: *Did you ever hear of Walt Whitman before?*

WOMAN: *Yeah, when I was in school we had to memorize some of his poems, but I forgot them now.*

AC: *So the greatest poet of freedom . . .*

WOMAN: *He lived there?*

AC: *Yeah.*

Camden, New Jersey, across the street from Walt Whitman's house. These women are "talking" to their loved ones in the prison the state saw fit to build across from the poet's house.

WOMAN: *It's funny how they put a jail right across from his house, right? Where they say all the bad people go. But these people aren't bad, though. Like my boyfriend is in there just 'cause this guy said, "Yeah, that's the guy who shot my brother." But, I mean, people try to say that they different from people on the outside, but they the same people like the people out here. They just the ones that get caught.*

Whitman's prophecies, Ginsberg's lamentations, Kerouac's lyric of the open road . . . they all flow into the signing of these women speaking to their caged loves. "Are you making a study of communication?" one of the girls asked. "Yes," I said. And miscommunication.

"I have met many communicators in my life, but you are some of the best!" I told them. I meant it, too.

THE land of the free and the brave leads the world in incarcerating its citizens.

How free are the rest of us on the outside?

Utopias: The Bruderhof, Oneida, Niagara Falls

I MET a boy on a country road in California about twenty years ago who carried a tattered copy of Whitman's *Leaves of Grass* in the pocket of his peacoat. We were hitchhiking in different directions but had plenty of time (there was plenty of time in those days) so we sat and talked for a while. He told me he had heard of a commune in northern California where everyone lived on fruit and went about naked. He was on his way there, sure of acceptance. Being of a more cynical disposition, I told him that, no doubt, everyone there *was* fruit, and that they weren't long for this world.

In truth, I was only a shade less trusting than he was. I was myself on the way to a community of utopians in northern California who were strict vegetarians and did go about naked most of the time. They were also accepting of strangers, and without guile. When a car stopped, the boy gave me his only possession, the tattered *Leaves of Grass*. I carried it with me to my friends' commune and I spent many hours lying naked on a patch of grass, reading Whitman out loud to my naked comrades. Whitman saw himself being read precisely in this way in some future golden age. He saw himself being passed "from hand to hand," in a book "that fits in your pocket." (What pocket if you're naked?)

"I am better with the reader in the open air," he wrote.

Twenty years and an age have passed since then. Today, when I want to run away I want to run to my *past.* Alas! There is a book full of places to run away to, a kind of utopian black book I keep hidden behind a loose brick in the basement. It's called *Intentional Communities: A Guide to Cooperative Living.* It's a book of communes, hundreds of them, all over the United States. It is surprising to see that there are still so many active communes left in the 1990s. The conventional wisdom is that after the sixties everybody was poured into a suit behind a desk and forced to live with a mate in front of a TV set. It certainly seemed that way to me, because all the communes I knew back in those mythical days broke up on the jagged rocks of poverty, jealousy, and whose turn it was to wash the dishes.

Not so, according to this directory. If your taste is for the simple life and you like plants, for instance, you can join the Adirondack Herbs community, where you can gather medicines, work with bees and greenhouses, and eat vegetarian food. If you think feeding the homeless is a good idea, there is Casa Maria in Milwaukee. For the Platonic groves of philosophy there is the Krotona Institute in Ojai, California. If you love the pleasures of the flesh, check out the Kerista society in San Francisco: they practice orthodox polyfidelity—whatever that is. Almost all of these utopias and would-be utopias are located in or near paradise.

Looking at the map, I see that every state has communes except Utah. I'm sure that there are communes in Utah but maybe their lifestyle philosophies are too startling to be listed here. There is also no word in the book on what any of these places do about washing dishes. But it's reassuring that they are still around. It means that not everyone in this country is in the army, in school, or in prison. State communism may be dead but the communal urge is not. A friend of mine, once a commune addict, now a software designer, told me wistfully: "It's not the high principles I miss . . . it's the smell of soy and cayenne . . . and the pitter-patter of many naked feet in the morning." In other words, the comfort of a family. A different family.

AFTER visiting Whitman, I turned the prow of my boat onto a road that runs through one of the most mysterious areas in North America: a narrow section of western New York where utopias have consistently taken hold since the mid-nineteenth century. Along this psychic highway, in the area known as the Burned-Over Patch, there flourished the Shakers, the Oneida Community, the Mormons, and dozens of other expressions of the American transcendental urge that Whitman also embodied. This is where Joseph Smith found the gold tablets with the Book of Mormon inscribed on them.

They called this area the Burned-Over Patch "because of the frequency with which the fires of the revival spirit swept through the region," said one commentator.

The Bruderhof

THE Bruderhof community was founded by refugees from Hitler's Germany. They are Christian communists and pacifists who trace their beliefs to the sixteenth century, like the Hutterites, the Mennonites, and the Amish. Nine hundred souls dedicated to the childlike love of Jesus live in this village.

> KLAUS MEIER, Bruderhof elder: *All the members of this community have declared themselves without any private property, and all we have, all what you see here, all the buildings, the factory, the dining room, belongs to God. I would say that I have nothing. I don't want any property for myself. Because I think that the property, the private property, leads to social injustice, and that leads to war.*

> AC: *I grew up in Romania, under state communism, that used all the words of community and of brotherhood, but they didn't mean that. It meant that the power was all in the hands of the state. So all my life I looked for someplace or some people for whom those words were real.*

> HANS MEIER, Klaus's father, one of the Bruderhof founders: *Community is an expression of our life, simply. Because it is love your neighbor as yourself, that is the equivalent to love your God. And if you love your neighbor as yourself, you share with him.*

Lunch and dinner are communal here. Breakfast is taken with one's family—but some families are as numerous as small communities. The community is immersed in itself, continually on guard against the outside. All the telephones are internal. No one is allowed to watch television or listen to the radio. News of the world is excerpted from the newspapers by the elders and posted on the schoolhouse wall.

I feel like an encyclopedia of dangerous knowledge in here, a seed-pod filled with the ill winds of my time.

Communal dinner at the Bruderhof community. Not a
four-star kitchen.

KLAUS: *In this community we all want to be like the members of one*
organism; the eye does its work and the mouth does its work, but they
are part of a body, they don't consider themselves higher or lower, in
fact they don't think at all.

I sat with Klaus's father, Hans, who is ninety-two years old, on a
bench outside the toy factory. A young Christian doctor from a nearby

The history of time according to Bruderhof beliefs. Time ends in 1975. I visited them in posthistory.

town sat with us. The doctor spoke about the idea of service, and Christ's original intentions, and then added: "In the beginning of the Church no soldiers or judges were allowed to become Christians." Hans, who had been a pacifist all his life, said that there were good reasons for that, but that currently the community faced two more urgent problems, namely the way in which the children just grab their food at dinner now instead of waiting for the elders to be served first, and secondly, the tendency to sneak "unwholesome spices into the food itself."

The food at Bruderhof seems designed to suppress any hint of sensuality. At lunch, I chewed two tiny and cold fried saltless schnitzels surrounded by two depressed cauliflower florets, and noted that the food plate went by at breakneck speed, followed anxiously by several hundred pairs of eyes. I never had a chance at the severe hard rolls in the handwoven basket. For dessert, a square brown compound landed in front of me, and when I didn't eat it, I could feel that it wouldn't go to waste. A very old woman next to me rubbed her gums together

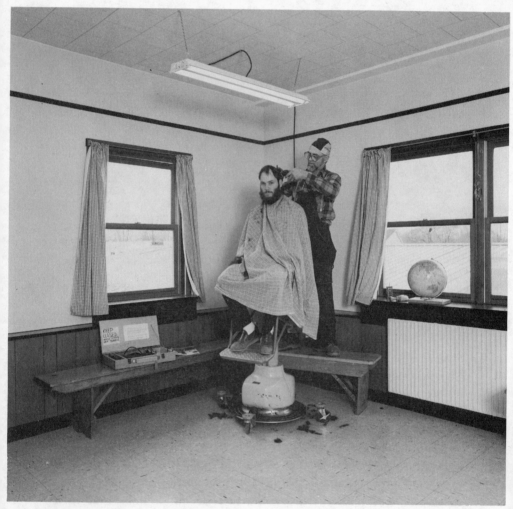

But it's free.

audibly. I wondered what these good Christians would have thought of our commune in northern California and the curry-laced bowls of luscious vegetables that we ate with our bare fingers in delicious anticipation of erotomaniac postprandial *frissons*.

These are some of the Bruderhof principles:

being poor in spirit
not divorcing your wife (or husband)
not swearing oaths (including allegiance ones)
giving away your cloak
going the second mile
loving your neighbor
and your enemy
not laying up treasure on earth

Not getting a funny haircut is not one of the principles.

The community's business—making children's toys and equipment for the handicapped—has made the Bruderhof wealthy. It's a painful paradox for these believers in voluntary poverty. Now and then when they feel that they have acquired too many things they bring these things to the village square and make a great sacrificial mound that is given away.

There was no surplus when I was growing up. One day our next-door neighbors in Romania broke into our kitchen with axes and communalized our living quarters. I cringe involuntarily amid all these seemingly happy communards and wonder—remembering—if they feel like I did as a child—about going to the bathroom, about being seen at all times, about the fear of giving away my thoughts. We would have wallowed in the comfort that the Bruderhoff fear will lead to moral corruption.

The love of small children is evident throughout the community. I'm not so sure about the adolescents who go to public schools outside the village but whose thoughts are open to the scrutiny of the elders.

When two young people become attracted to one another they must tell the elders, who decide if they are indeed suitable. They are then considered engaged but cannot even hold hands until they are married.

We are no longer in MTV America, that's for sure.

I asked the kids about music, clothes, records, dances, new shoes, the American teenage essentials.

TEEN 1: *I think those things, they're not really necessary. You want them, but you can live without them.*

TEEN 2: *We're used to our way of life, they have a different way of life, and they accept it, we accept it.*

I also asked them about dating and attractions to the opposite sex.

TEEN 1: *I don't know of any boy that's ever felt attracted to me, but when I feel attracted to a boy I just try and not show it because there's nothing . . . I won't . . . it won't . . . there's nothing I can do about it.*

Earlier Klaus Meier had said: "In America, I love the freedom. But the fear about this freedom is that people use it for to satisfy their own desires." The teenager can do nothing about it because an old man fears the freedom of modern America.

Adolescence, the essence of embarrassment! While I was talking with the young people, an elder who was listening to us admonished them: "Speak of Jesus or it's meaningless!" I bet. God forbid they should inadvertently succumb to a rock star younger than Jesus. Adherence to the community is voluntary. Members "commit" when they are old enough. But I wonder how easily one can break away from this safe world tucked away within its cocoon of faith. Even the pleasures of gossip are forbidden. "We do not speak about one another behind our backs." Everything is in the open, and what isn't is not articulated.

Still, listen to how good it sounds (if all was just the way it sounds): *"There is no law but that of love (II John 5–6). Love means having joy in others. Then what does being annoyed with them mean? Words of love convey the joy we have in the presence of brothers and sisters. By the same token it is out of the question to speak about a Brotherhood member in a spirit of irritation and vexation. There must never be talk, either in open remarks or by insinuation, against a brother or a sister . . . under no circumstances beyond a person's back. Direct address is the only way possible."* So wrote the founder of the Bruderhof, Eberhard Arnold, on October 13, 1935, in a pamphlet entitled "The Childlike Spirit."

The freedom to live so severely has chilled me. And yet I like these ascetic missionaries from another time. I could not live in their world—and they would never care to live in mine. In fact, I don't even care to speculate on the intensity of possible mutual shocks. Still, application of their "no gossip" rule to modern American life would eliminate the following classes of people: lawyers, politicians, policemen, agents (literary, theatrical, and secret), and bored housewives. And the following prevailing phenomena: television, movies, office scuttlebutt. That wouldn't be such a bad thing.

THE utopians along the "psychic highway" established their communities in response to many of the questions that trouble us today. Americans in the latter part of the nineteenth century were like us—in many ways. Jacksonian prosperity—achieved in part by ruthless dispossession of Native Americans, was followed by the Civil War, and then by an accelerated technological revolution. Like us, they felt keenly the passing of nature, the breakdown of families and familiar values, and the alienation of workers in the cities. Millennial fervor swept among them, bringing them news of the end of the world and the coming of Christ.

> *Things are in the saddle,*
> *And ride mankind.* (Emerson)

The nineteenth century was an articulate age. Its articulateness tended simultaneously upward and downward. It attempted to explain and rationalize primary desires, hoping to harness them by bringing them to light. But these desires are the very ones that escape articulation, particularly sex and transcendence. Faced with their intractability the utopian hunters of the nineteenth century either fell back on simple faith like the Old Testamentarian Jesus of Bruderhof, or renounced desire altogether like the Shakers.

Oneida

BETTY WHELAN and Robert Friedman are direct descendants of John Humphrey Noyes, the founder of Oneida. For thirty-two years, between 1848 and 1879, a radical experiment in social organization took place on these grounds under Noyes's leadership.

> *The thing we have done for which we are called "Free Lovers," is simply this: We have left the simple form of marriage and advanced to the complex stage of it. We have no quarrel with those who believe in exclusive dual marriage and faithfully observe it, but we have concluded that for us there is a better way. The honor and faithfulness that constitutes an ideal marriage may exist between two hundred as well as two; while the guarantees for women and children are much greater in the Community than they can be in any private family.*

> *Oneida Community Handbooks,* 1867 and 1871

The Oneida mansion, surrounded by big trees, shaking in the wind, steady in its neoclassical yearning, was a monument to the mysterious disappearance of articulation, the articulation that attempted to explain the unexplainable.

The Oneida Perfectionists believed that Christ had already come and that we now live in paradise—so there ought to be neither sin nor guilt among the children of God. For thirty-two years the Oneida communitarians practiced sexual liberty in a form known as "complex marriage." The atmosphere at Oneida is said to have been one of continual flirtation as in a medieval court of love. They were prosperous and lived together in the Oneida Mansion where many of their wealthy descendants live today.

I feel that they were happy. Sleeping in a narrow bed in a small but airy room, I dream of Pre-Raphaelite women floating past me in diaphanous shimmer. Eventually they put me to sleep (although I think I'm already sleeping) but not before I feel an excruciating pain like the blade of a knife. "It's the red-eyed jealousy of men whose wives

Robert Friedman and Betty Whelan, direct descendants of Oneida's founder John Humphrey Noyes. Still sparkly at a venerable age, the two of them may credit their vitality to "stirpiculture," a form of genetic selection.

are tending to me" is my first thought. My second, as I fall doubly asleep: "Beautiful women make me sleepy."

The Victorian despair that produced Sigmund Freud is palpable in these rooms. Christ is notably absent. The portraits on the walls are those of Calliope, Pindar, Horace, Thalia, Polymnia, Zeno, Plato, Pythagoras, Clio, Socrates, Homer, Virgil, and Sappho. Listening to a concert in the Great Hall must have been an ecstatic experience, as everyone lived the music in expectation of a night of love and mystery. I sit in the deeply shaded gazebo on the mansion ground, and feel presences everywhere. A train is coming soon, bringing visitors (thousands came to visit Oneida when a train station was built) and there is great excitement.

Men practiced "male continence," an amazingly successful form of birth control that also gave women sexual satisfaction. The Oneidans frowned on romantic love and they broke up couples who became too intimate. Reproduction was a matter decided by the elders, who chose what they called "matched natures" for parenting. It was a practice they called "stirpiculture," an early form of eugenics. The Stirpiculture Committee approved who would have children with whom. Between 1869 and 1879 forty-five children were conceived this way. The children were raised apart from their parents in the Children's House, where they received careful schooling meant to break down age-old stereotypes between boys and girls. The communards practiced mutual criticism and self-criticism openly.

Betty and Robert are very old but there is an undeniable spark in their eyes, and they speak joyfully in defense of a long-past experiment. Oneida is a rich community now—Oneida silver is famous everywhere. At Roger's prompting, I ask Robert what it feels like to be the result of a eugenics experiment, like Hitler's. "Well, I'm not a very good example of it," Robert tells me. "These experiments were conceived in love, they were not racial like Hitler's." But the question has visibly unsettled Betty, who looks, for a brief moment, her ninety-some years.

Later, she and I take a walk to the Oneida cemetery, where are buried many of the children and grandchildren of John Humphrey Noyes. Betty walks beautifully straight, with the gait of a much younger woman. A sweet wind, a sort of *mistral* or *foehn*, the wind said to bring melancholy and cause suicide, is blowing over the graves. "It's not such a great thing to live this long," Betty says wistfully. "Things hurt, you forget things, people you know are long gone." And yet she exudes a childlike happiness, the mysterious certainty of an age completely out of reach to my cynical, quickly disappointed contemporaries. I think of other joyous old people I know, the poets James Broughton, Carl Rakosi . . . They all have it. Perhaps the dream of community, the love of beauty, interest in others instead of oneself is the secret of longevity.

Could I have lived in the Oneida Community? Probably not. Their "eugenics" experiment for one thing seems to have been meant for an

ethnically homogeneous group of Anglo-Saxons. Not a Jew among
them. And yet . . .

Niagara Falls

WHEN the Oneida Community broke up from internal and external
pressures—the good citizens of the state of New York were distressed
by the sexual goings-on—they went to Niagara Falls, "the second

*At Niagara Falls, the man who escaped all restraints is
imprisoned by tourism.*

biggest disappointment in a newly married American woman's life," as Oscar Wilde called the rushing water.

People dream of barreling into oblivion down here. People have strange ambitions. Ironically, there are plenty of sexual goings-on at Niagara but not of the sort Oneidans would have liked. Their taste ran to classical music, drama, and ancient poets and philosophers, not to a low-class circus of magicians, palm readers, acrobats, escape artists, and barrel riders, Ripley's and Houdini's worlds.

"The Houdini museum has literally spellbound thousands of people. The incomparable $100,000 Houdini Handcuff collection, the Steel Trunk used by Houdini in effecting his most dangerous Water Escape, the Amazing Psycho, Herman's Decapitation, the equipment used for Cutting A Girl of 8 In Half . . ." so says the brochure of the Houdini Museum.

The Oneidans would have also frowned on the honeymooners coupled so deliberately with one another—amid sprays, cheap neon, chintz, and kitsch—not a thought in their heads for community, alternative family systems, the millennial hope or "scientific propagation."

I rented a cheap bridal suite in a cheap motel ("2 nights/$49/soap provided by the management") and spent the evening in a red heart-shaped bathtub thinking about the differences between the severe Bruderhoff and the pleasure-loving Oneidans. If Hans Meier could have seen me now he would have been sure the devil had got in me. But the devil is in both of us, Hans. The pride of excess is equal to the pride of self-denial. Private bad taste is a special kind of grace.

*She will take your picture as you go over the Falls in a
barrel, but what she really wants is to run away with
someone in a Cadillac.*

I do—but who'll believe me?

Motor City

I DROVE across the Ambassador Bridge to Detroit. Huge trucks roared past me, paying no attention to my white knuckles. Equally distressed beside me was the very valiant Jean de Segonzac, holding on to his $100,000 camera for dear life. "If you plunge us to our deaths," he said with grim Gaelic humor, "I will kill you. It's not myself I care about, it's the camera!" I had noticed already that Jean cared little for his life, but treated his camera like a tender baby. He thought nothing of plunging from a cliff to get a shot. Once he got to the bottom, however, he shouted to his assistant, Chris, to lower his camera down as gently as possible. When she did, he cursed her for unnecessary roughness. There is something touchingly insane about a Frenchman with a camera. I think the French believe God gave Lumière the camera the way He gave Moses the tablets. Consequently, they see themselves as the new Chosen People.

As I drove on toward Detroit, where the landscape was dotted with the names of French explorers who had fought alongside the Indians against the English, Jean became more and more French.

HERE is my first American home, Detroit, where I lived between 1966 and 1968 and learned the first lessons of America. I learned the difference between "buy" and "ride," when I said to the driver of the Dexter bus, "Can I buy the Dexter bus?" and he said, "Go buy the Livernois bus!" and slammed the door shut. I took my newfound knowledge to the Wayne State cafeteria and wrote on girls' arms: "Ride the Dexter bus!" and they giggled and asked me if I was a

Communist spy. I was definitely a spy. This was, after all, Detroit, where the French doctor and writer Louis-Ferdinand Céline came in the 1930s to tend to Mr. Henry Ford's emaciated auto workers. Another literary spy.

This is Detroit, where I learned English, met Alice, took LSD, and saw the angry flames of the 1968 riots engulfing downtown. Alice was at the wheel; we were racing at the bottom of the terrifying cement tub that is the John Lodge Expressway. After we heard on the radio that the riots had broken out, I was sure that urban warriors hurling gasoline bombs would appear on the cement parapets above us and send us to a fiery death. As Jose Feliciano urged us to *Götterdämmerung* ("Light My Fire") and the downtown sky took on the red of flames, we emerged from the tunnel into our neighborhood, which had become a war zone. Our neighbors reeled about with bottles of liquor from looted stores. A party of sorts was going on. It was short-lived. The tanks of the National Guard soon appeared, pointing their guns at our apartment buildings. And firing at anyone sticking their heads out the window after curfew. The MC5 sang joyously: "Motor City's Burning! Motor City's Burning!," while another kamikaze-rock group, the Up, was howling at the police, "I Wanna Be Your Dog!"

Motown

DETROIT had it good in the days before the 1967 riots. The music was playing in what is now the Motown Museum, and was then just Motown. Obie Benson of the Four Tops was singing and Marv Johnson, the first artist whose songs were released by Motown, was at the keyboards.

MARV: *"I Love the Way You Love." Now, that's um, you could hear the spiritualism in that song.*

OBIE: *That was our souls coming out of here. I mean, and nothing stopped it, not even the hum of the machines.*

Detroit. Burn, baby, burn!

If these machines could talk, they would remember the magic voices of Diana Ross, Stevie Wonder, Michael Jackson, Marvin Gaye, Smokey Robinson, and so many others.

OBIE: *This music was everything, people could relate to it, they were proud. See, and when that music left, it's just like the automobiles leaving here now. See, no matter what people say, they might complain, but they're proud of that. See, this is something that I think is being taken out of a lot of people, they're not proud of anything.*

Motown gave Motor City as much pride as the car factories . . . and then one day—like everything else in Detroit—Motown up and left the soil of its soul and took off for the money and glitz of Hollywood.

OBIE: *People felt betrayed because Motown was like, everybody felt part of Motown because it was like, it was theirs. Everybody here is*

Rodin's "The Thinker," Detroit Art Museum. In 1967 we
urged him to get off his ass and do something. It's 1991—he's
still thinking.

proud of Motown, it's theirs, and when they left here it was almost like
losing one of your family. Being rejected.

MOTOWN wasn't the only bright light to abandon Detroit. The Pistons
left Cobo Arena for the greener hoops of the suburbs. The science
museum closed; public libraries shut down; Amtrak trains don't stop at

the station anymore; even Rodin's "Thinker" wonders what happened to the Detroit Institute of Art, which can only afford to stay open a few hours a day. Between 1950 and 1987 Detroit lost 40 percent of its population. During the decade after the riots of 1967, the city lost one-third of its jobs. Even Henry Ford's original car plant assembles only ghosts now. On "Devil's Night" before Halloween the rabble rages through the streets, setting fire to whatever is left. "Motor City" is now known as "Murder City."

Amid the empty parking lots of the downtown riverfront rises an ominous structure. Feudal lords in the Middle Ages built themselves huge fortified castle to keep out the rabble. The "Renaissance Center" looks built for the same reason. It stands in the middle of the devastated city, a monument to the civic mind gone haywire. What renaissance? The interior of this fortress was designed by Kafka. The endless circles don't lead anywhere. There must be people lost here since it was first built—looking for the exit.

There isn't any exit from Detroit.

The People Mover

JUST outside the Renaissance Center, I enter another insane volute of the city brain: mass transit to nowhere. A train called "people mover" (which has been called variously "a dogless tail," and "a horizontal elevator to nowhere") goes past a city that looks like Dresden after the bombing. By the time it opened in 1987, this $200.3 million boondoggle was two years late, $60 million over budget, and barely anyone was left to ride it. A woman named Jill Demaris, a pastel-clad suburban enthusiast who founded a surreally named outfit named Detroit Upbeat, points out the vacant lots and burnt buildings and trills excitedly: "See all the development opportunities? The renovation potential? The riverfront choices?" I see. I see that when a city becomes extinct, its last inhabitants go crazy.

When I lived here people sat on their porches and talked. The descendants of Polish, Ukrainian, Romanian, German, and Irish immigrants who came here to work in the car factories lived noisily in their neighborhoods. The black sections of the town teemed with life. Even during the riots there was a certain camaraderie on the streets—until, of course, the tanks of the 82nd and 101st Airborne divisions showed up on Woodward Avenue. There are no tanks now: only unemployment, poverty, and fear stalk these streets. A soldier returned here from the Persian Gulf War and was gunned down next to his house by a robber.

There are no people—only sculptures of people. I lived around here somewhere, next to the house where Charles Lindbergh was born. It's all gone now, kidnapped like Lindbergh's baby.

On the Cadillac Assembly Line

THE Cadillac assembly plant isn't yet closed, however, so I decide to take my Caddy back to his mommy for a visit. Security precautions at the plant make the prisons of New Jersey look like a piece of cake. There are metal detectors, armed guards, a big white line that can't be crossed, special badges, bulletproof control booths. After what seems like several days, I am cleared to enter the Caddy sanctum, provided that I stay on the right side of the painted line, do not speak with the workers, and look only in the direction approved by the guide. The Gestapo-like guide has already classified me as a dangerous pinko liberal on account of my involuntary irreverence.

Since the movie *Roger & Me*, the top brass at General Motors has issued draconian edicts against outsiders. We enter a constructivist hell of rail lines, overhead trains, revolving compartments, drawers, sub-drawers, screws, and twisting appendages, from which hang the workers—mere appendages themselves in a vast, clanking geometry of boredom. An enormous American flag hangs over the assembly room. The guide proudly tells me that only a few days ago, General Colin Powell, fresh from the Gulf, and his Soviet counterpart, fresh from hell, addressed thousands of workers at the plant.

"About what?" I ask her. She looks at me astonished and peeved. "What do you think?" she says sourly. "About these poor workers who look like parts of parts of parts fitting holes into holes into holes?" I try, tentatively. She pierces me with a gaze of pure GM alloy. "About the New World Order." Oh, that. She also tells me that every morning the workers have to listen to a Japanese-style pep talk. "It must be very inspiring!" I say.

When I leave the plant, I buy *The Detroit News*. The headline says, "GM WIELDS AX: 74,000 JOBS CUT." By 1995 GM will eliminate 20,000 salaried and 54,000 hourly positions. Welcome to the New World Order!

When Mr. Henry Ford introduced the assembly line to his factory and invented the modern world, diverse people cheered. Even the Communists thought that the workers' paradise was now at hand. Among the Communists who paid homage to this capitalist panacea was Diego Rivera. His mural stands on a wall at the (mostly closed now) Detroit Museum of Art, testifying to a gentler, kinder time. His workers are clean, his bosses look human, the coming world of the industrial utopia is hopeful. Nothing was going to stop the march to safe labor and full employment!

The GM parking lot is self-consciously full of thousands of American cars. Anyone foolish enough to park a Japanese car here wouldn't find much of it on return. My Caddy doesn't have that problem: it glides past its grandchildren with the grand air of a dowager.

The Fist

JOE LOUIS, heavyweight boxing champ, had his fist immortalized by artist Robert Graham in downtown Detroit. The city fathers were hard put to decide in what direction this twenty-four-foot steel fist should thrust. Fearing the symbolism of directing it toward the white suburbs, they pointed it at Canada. They should have pointed it at City Hall.

The fist of Joe Louis, heavyweight boxing champ, pointing at Canada. Blame Canada for the ills of Detroit.

The Tire

HOVERING near the Detroit Metropolitan Airport is a huge Uniroyal tire, about which my friend Jeffrey Miller said, "It's big enough a family can live in it." The Uniroyal plant in Detroit closed in the early 1980s. Uniroyal/Goodrich has been bought out by Michelin.

The Guytons: Souls of Detroit

IN the middle of the desert great big flowers bloom sometimes. Tyree and Karen Guyton, and Tyree's grandfather Sam Mackey, are three of these flowers. They've taken the bleak world around them and turned it to color. The discarded trash of the urban nightmare has been transformed: there are bicycles, toys, football helmets, baseball cards, broken appliances, bent birdcages, Christmas-tree lights, and shoes . . . hundreds of shoes . . . Tyree and Karen have laid down shoes on the street among the hulks of abandoned buildings.

KAREN: *You wonder who wore these shoes? Where are these people now? What are they doing? Are they alive? Where are they? Are they misplaced? Are they homeless? So, this has a lot to do with the plight of these people. So that's why we call it "Street People."*

There is a grave here where Tyree and Karen buried the soul of two abandoned houses that they transformed with their art. The city of Detroit left fifteen thousand vacant buildings standing. They bulldozed Tyree and Karen's houses.

TYREE: *Six years of my life, they came over, and in thirty minutes they took that away.*

AC: *That's what they did in the Communist country where I grew up. They bulldozed art that wasn't approved by the state. They just brought in the bulldozers.*

In the kitchen of the small house on Heidelberg Street on Detroit's East Side, Grampa Sam sits at a table drawing big colored pictures. Across from him is a neighborhood kid who draws, too, encouraged by the old man, who laughs, quotes the Bible, and encompasses whoever looks at him with a warm, loving gaze. Kids come to the Guytons' house all the time to make art. There are crayons and paper for them. The creative spirit has burst out of the paper, though, and climbed the walls, the chairs, and the furniture. . . .

Detroit's Tree of Life, part of Karen and Tyree Guyton's
"Heidelberg Project."

The Heidelberg Project (what splendid irony in a city devastated by the weapons of neglect!) had been going on five years, until November 23, 1991, when, without prior notification, bulldozers and wrecking crews came and tore down four houses that the Guytons had transformed with their art. The day I visited Tyree and Karen and Grampa Guyton the state of Michigan just cut thousands of people off welfare rolls. The day after my visit, a judge found the Guytons guilty of littering and ordered them to remove all the shoes from the street.

There was an international outcry when the city demolished the Guytons' houses. French museums offered to display their drawings, photographs, and assemblages. But the Guytons are not very interested in the chic aspects of their activities. They stubbornly persist in trans-

*Sam Mackey, Tyree Guyton's grandfather. He gave me a
drawing, made at the kitchen table. Grampa Mackey loved
kids who wandered in off the street to draw with him. He
died at the age of ninety-four, on June 26, 1992, not long
after this picture was taken.*

forming Heidelberg Street. Speaking with them, I get the feeling that
I am in the presence of a True Vision. The love that underlies their
mission expresses itself in "art," but it aims for something more, the
reestablishment of paradise on earth, perhaps. After all, Mr. and Mrs.
Blake sat naked in their postage-stamp garden in the middle of London, the most polluted city of the nineteenth century, and proclaimed
themselves to be in Eden. The Guytons' realm is bigger than the
Blakes', but the surrounding hells are comparable.

Jim Gustafson and Other Friends

HELL is not without its heroes. Most of my old friends are gone now, either dead or relocated to the coasts. But some persist, and like Tyree and Karen Guyton, try to wrest some joy from the bleakness, make life decent, perhaps even beautiful. People like my friend Jim Gustafson, who stayed in Detroit to write poetry. Jim acts tough, like one of Elmore Leonard's streetwise punks, but underneath he's all raw tenderness like twilight in a smoky "blind pig." Blind pigs are where the restless souls of Detroit go after all the bars close. Hidden behind unmarked façades, the blind pigs throb with sorrowful urban blues. Jim best captured Detroit in the lines: "Detroit just lies there/Like the head of a dog on a platter."

The evening we got together, at Alvin's bar, he seemed just like my old friend Jim from our San Francisco days, when we roamed the streets looking for free drinks. We recited our poetry out loud to whoever would buy us some. We were young and terrible in those days. When Jim left San Francisco and moved back to his hometown, I feared for him. Detroit grinds down the sensitive like sausage. Those who leave do not return. Those who cannot leave kill themselves. Not long before I saw Jim, one of Detroit's finest painters, Bradley Jones, had committed suicide.

If Jim seemed the same at the beginning of the evening, by its end it was apparent that he was not. I had asked him to read his poem about Detroit, but when he took the stage at Alvin's, he threw his book away, and began what sounded like a choked lament and eulogy to his youth and mine. He'd had too much. Too much emotion from our reunion, too much poetry, too much Jack Daniel's. He pitched forward and fell off the stage with a thunderous sound like a bulldozed house. He crashed spectacularly, like Detroit.

He was, miraculously, unscathed. It was a poet's fall but it was not the fiery crash of Icarus: it was the dusty collapse of *fin-de-siècle* Midwest. I had seen Jim create a number of disturbances, minor and major, at poetry readings and art events over the years, in many cities. But while I knew just how entertaining he could be, the audiences were never sure. This time, however, there was no mistaking his fall.

Jim Gustafson ("Jimbo"), Detroit poet, friend.

He hadn't planned it. To his credit, our great cameraman, Monsieur Jean de Segonzac, never stopped rolling.

I GAVE my first public reading in Detroit in 1966. The event was sponsored by the Artists' Workshop, an underground music and poetry group. On the unreadable psychedelic poster done in swirls of color my name was listed at the bottom below the MC5, the world's loudest rock 'n' roll band; the Up, another loud and angry band; Jerry Younkins, the man with the longest hair in Detroit; and a score of others I don't remember. After my name, it said: "French poet." I had decided at the time that "Romanian" was too strange for the ears of my American friends.

I read on the roof of a building on John Lodge in a language I think was some sort of incipient English, but it hardly mattered. The long-haired audience was so happily stoned that I am sure they understood every ripple of meaning. Later that evening I couldn't hear anything; my ears had stopped working. Inside my head, there was a tidal wave of sound and the primal repetitions of the MC5's famous tune, "Kick out the jams, motherfucker!," as well as snippets of the Up's "I Wanna Be Your Dog." One of their later hits said appropriately: "It's 1969, and I Don't Care!" Well, it was 1967, and I cared enormously, immensely, so much in fact that I didn't care at all. It was amazing to be alive.

AT Alvin's in 1991, before the Crash of Jim, the crowd was warm but infinitely more polite. I have always loved the people of Detroit. Midwesterners, in general. They shoot straight. I have lived on both coasts and I always made friends there with refugees from the Midwest. The poetry reading began with Ken Mikolowski, one of my oldest friends here, who seized the microphone to read his spare, ironic commentaries. He was followed by Mick Vranich, his face carved out of some kind of granite, who performed harsh urban indictments. "Don't look at me, look at your TV!" he shouted.

When at last Jim Gustafson's turn came, what was in his heart never made it to his lips.

Who Lives Here

THE Midwest is home to a stubborn humanity. It takes grit and endurance to persist here. And faith—that spring will come. A stern ethic reigns here, a puritanical rigor, a black-and-white sparseness, a necessity to conserve. You save your breath here; you can't afford to waste words or heat. People like Jim are a necessary corrective to the rigors of this place. How far my lush, loamy, rich, sexy, corrupt, chatty South seems! We may all be exiles only from the weather. Heat—or the lack of it—may be what makes you feel at home or not at home.

Detroit.
Tabula rasa.

Detroit Love Song

FOR my Detroit friends: the Incomparable Derelict, Jim
Gustafson; the Impeccable Ken Mikolowski; the Joyful Ann
Mikolowski; the Wind-Hewn-Rock-Honest Mick Vranich;
and Roy "Flame-Keeper" Castlebury.

Detroit gave me my first America.
19 years old and scared I watched cars flow over John Lodge
  Expressway
and decided that they followed a law The Law of Cars
by which blue cars followed blue cars red cars red cars and so
  on.
I stood over the bridge there that cold March evening of 1966
  in my immigrant-green thin nylon Romanian coat
  & shivered watching the car river

wondering why I had come
who I was
was I always going to be this skinny
was I ever going to get laid?

And at the Wayne State Univ. cafeteria I tried talking with my
    hands
    to girls who mostly wouldn't talk to me
    and when they did I wrote
    in gratitude & abjection
lines of poetry on their arms and if they let me on their
    shoulders
& one or two let me write a poem all over them
& those were my happiest days
& those were my best poems

And on the second floor of that Wayne State Univ. cafeteria
    that is no more
at the Lost & Found counter
    worked my future wife Alice
but I didn't know it yet
& walked instead relentlessly nervously walked
    without peace over the big boulevards and into strange
    neighborhoods
& past the burnt shells of factories
looking for the center of the city
wondering where the center of the city could be
    because I could not imagine a city without a center—
    that was inconceivable to me—
    a center where everyone met, talked, & maybe found love—
& when I asked people pointed me to shopping centers
    and malls and central offices
    & more shopping centers
& there was no sign of people meeting & talking in one place
    no sign of love—
& because my English was lousy I was always misunderstood
& when I said to the driver of the Dexter bus:
    "Can I buy this bus?"
    meaning "Can I ride it?"
    he shoved me rudely & said:
    "Go buy the Livernois bus!"
    & still no love
        & no center—

until the Trans-Love Energies commune on John Lodge!
A sign there said:
   "C'mon people love one another right now!"
& I went there & there was music & long-haired guys
   & girls mostly girls
   & they wore long skirts
   & had big dreamy sixties eyes that were just opening
      wide out of the sleep of America
   & that's how the psychedelic sixties
   came to Detroit & to me
   & to the world Thank God
   & the gray March drizzle turned party-colored
   & I got rid of my immigrant-green pitiful nylon coat
   & let my hair grow and wore an amulet around my neck
   & took LSD
   which put me firmly & finally in the world
      & allowed me to belong in it
   & not only that
   but one evening while in love with the world
   & waiting for the bus
   & having an odd powerful physical sensation that the planet
      even in Detroit
         kept surging unimpeded through plants & animals
         & things—
I saw a vision of beauty in the form of two girls coming toward
   me—

& I read to them from the book in my hand
   which was Howl *by Allen Ginsberg*
& they took me to hear the Muddy Waters Blues Band
   at the Chessmate Club
& one of those girls was Alice
   who worked at Lost & Found
   who had a big yellow bed
   in her tiny apartment on West Ferry
   & a typewriter
   & she found me I guess
   & then I wasn't so lost—
I started typing on her typewriter the poetry of that party-
   colored universe which strangely now
      even in Detroit
         pulsed stronger & stronger

& I called the book when I finished it a week later:
Insane People with Beautiful Sidewalks
   for all the obvious reasons
& that was my first book in my new language & I was home.

Detroit gave me love & a center & music
   & a job at the Detroit Public Library
   where I rollerskated in search of books
   until one day I took some mescaline
   & rollerskated too long & too much & they fired me
   but that was OK
      because I knew a hundred people by then

      & we were all artists & writers & music-makers
& we wanted America out of Vietnam
& we wrote on the back of the "Thinker" by the Detroit Art Museum:
WHAT'S THIS PIG
   THINKING ABOUT?
THE TIME
   FOR REVOLUTION
    IS NOW!

And that was Detroit in 1966
   but by 1967 it was:
UP AGAINST THE WALL MOTHERFUCKER!
   & "C'mon Baby Light My Fire!"
    José Feliciano singing
& we turned around in the car to look
& downtown was in flames
   & then we had to lie on the floor
   of our artistic apartment
    full of collages & poetry
because there were tanks on Woodward Avenue
   & if they saw your head
   after curfew
they machine-gunned your building & killed you & everyone inside
   dead—
& that was Johnson's Great Society
& those tanks were elite U.S. troops
   from the 82nd & 101st Airborne divisions—

& things weren't so much fun after that
& those who didn't die then
   wanted to leave
& those who stayed
   died anyway after that
with a few exceptions
I see happily here—

& that was it
except for a few million other things
& a handful of lifelong friends
with whom in the strangeness of faraway cities
   on various oceans
we practiced stories of Detroit
   —like an exotic rite—
& it's true
   in a way I was born here
      born an American here
         an American without a car
            in Motor City
               born in Detroit oddly enough
                  but never regretfully—

Written on the occasion of the reading reunion at Alvin's in
Detroit, December 13, 1991.

Folk Tales

MAYOR KOZAREN rules Hamtramck, a Polish city in the heart of
Detroit. Seated under the portrait of Bobby Vinton, the Polish prince,
he tells me about all the presidents and famous people who have
visited his office.

There may not be many jobs left in the car factories, but the
descendants of the Eastern European immigrants who came here for
them can still find something to do.

There is only one way to subdue your nightmares: face them. If

Mayor Kozaren, the mayor of Hamtramck, Michigan, below
Bobby Vinton, the Polish prince. There are other (smaller)
luminaries on the walls: Gerald Ford, the Pope, Lech Walesa.

there is a hell for vegetarians, Kowalski's is the place. Huge steel vats
brim over with the gurgling innards of freshly snuffed pigs. Intestine
skins are blown wide open like the condoms of giants by machines that
stuff them full of chopped animal. The floor is a gooey mess on which
I go sliding, while attempting not to gag. Pig-skating, I think, pig-
skating as a new Olympic event. Everywhere I turn, a steel vat hisses
meaningfully, a freezer door opens, filled with the heads of pigs. I have

It's a living! Sausage maker at Kowalski's.

donned the Kowalski hat and white apron and I am following the manager down steel staircases with greasy banisters. I control my nausea with some difficulty but, clearly, if I were to throw up no one would notice. My vomit would be quickly absorbed within the guts and eyeballs of pigs. It stinks something awful. But even as I begin to envision great tours of meat eaters becoming vegetarians on the spot, I realize that the workers here are quite happy.

WORKER 1: *I work about twenty years here. This place . . . and I like this . . . this job.*

AC: *You know sausages inside out.*

WORKER 2: *I'm working for this company since 1964, I'm very happy you know—to help my children be somebody.*

There is something about all these particular Polish, Ukrainian, and Romanian butchers, something that wakes an indefinable dread in my Jewish blood. I really do hope their children become somebodies, educated somebodies hopefully, not the angry somebodies their parents and grandparents were once upon a depression and a war. In Romania before World War II the Iron Guard pulled thousands of Jews out of their beds in the middle of the night. They transported them in trucks to the stockyards in Bucharest. There they shot them and then hung them from meat hooks. They carved KOSHER into the flesh of their bodies.

The manager pulls a scared Romanian refugee from under a boiler in the underground room, which is lined wall to wall with huge freezers. The man, a short, stocky peasant with sweaty hair glued to his pocked narrow forehead, salutes me shyly and cowers. He begs me in whispers not to take his picture. He is confusing us with the Immigration Department. I reassure him. He tells me that he left just as "the butchers" had begun hunting people after the death of Ceauşescu. I'm not quite sure I understand, and then I do. The only men hunted in Romania after the execution of Ceauşescu in 1989 were the worst members of Securitate, the secret police. Only those charged with killing unarmed civilians were pursued at all. I can't swear to it, but if this man feared "the butchers," it was because he had been a "butcher" himself. And now he works among animal butchers, which is the first step to legitimacy. This possible monster has come here the same way that the butchers of World War II, the Nazis of Bucharest, had come a long time ago.

Even today, among the Eastern Europeans who came to America after the war, one can find a fair number of war criminals. The bishop of the Romanian church in Detroit, Bishop Trifa, was among those who participated in the slaughter of Jews at the stockyards. The U.S. government was in the process of trying to deport him when he died.

Farewell

THIS last farewell from Detroit was more sorrowful than the last. You have given me much, city of motors and neon sunsets, but have been rough on yourself. I should have held on to my memories, where you are always new, like America, gritty, tough, but inhabited—full of rude working life.

Seeing you like this broke my heart.

Bankrupt in Detroit. Things Goya never dreamt of. The sleep of the republic gives birth to the monsters of kitsch.

Chicago. The wealth of the land flows through her.

Chicago

IN 1967 I hitchhiked from Detroit to Chicago with my first American girlfriend, Gloria. She went on to Madison, Wisconsin, to be with her other boyfriend while I went to visit a literary hero of mine, the scholar of religions Mircea Eliade at the University of Chicago. Eliade was most kind to the skinny, nervous kid full of questions about the meanings of things.

The meaning of a rusting, decaying America was not among those questions. America's industrial might was not in question then, at the height of the Vietnam War; her industries were going full blast. Not long ago the machines of the future were made here, but before we could even understand it the future's become past.

Nothing ages faster than the future.

DRIVING is dreaming. . . . Maybe everything around me is just the congealed dream of a million drivers . . . the Industrial Age, a dream . . . a dream, the rusting ruins of machines . . . the vast Midwest that once fed the world and now weeps to herself, a dream too . . . migrants, salesmen, con artists, heartbroken poets all dreaming their way West.

THERE is an invisible border between the two great midwestern cities of Detroit and Chicago. Others may not notice it but I'm border-sensitive: I can feel one in the dark for thirty miles. Borders run hell-deep through the European mind, which may in fact be only a crisscross of barbed wire. For the long years of my uncertain immigrant status I was reluctant to cross even imaginary borders because I didn't have either a passport or a driver's license. I now have both.

Chicago, the city Carl Sandburg called "hog butcher to the world," has managed to keep its vigor and its boldness. Her buildings rise arrogantly out of an age of optimism, the age of brash early capitalism before taxes. A river of wealth flowed through her, an abundance that astonished the world. I can see vast fields of wheat and immense herds of cattle.

Chicago's totem pole: cars, our ancestors.

The First McDonald's

PROOF of the power of dreams: Ray Kroc, one man with a single idea, a rounded *idée fixe* called a hamburger, began to dream an empire and, lo and behold, one day the entire planet is covered by the mighty waves of his single thought. . . . If anybody's going to get to heaven it's Mr. Kroc on a ladder of billions of burgers, the number that most approaches infinity. Next to rock 'n' roll, McDonald's is the most enduring American creation of the second half of the twentieth century.

They are chomping them down in Moscow, Beijing, Des Moines, wearing them in Poughkeepsie and Frankfurt. . . . (SING THIS)

CHUCK, a company official, speaking of First McDonald's (now a museum): *This is the only early McDonald's restaurant that's been preserved exactly as it opened April 15, 1955. And these days the students who come through Hamburger University over at our McDonald's campus nearby come over to get a little feeling for the culture. It's really a cultural experience. It's a chance to see, touch, and feel what McDonald's was like in the beginning. Now we got for you an official McDonald's crew hat here just as was worn in the fifties. And we make you an honorary crew person.*

AC (pointing to life-sized replica of early McDonald's employee): *I could look like him, he's tall.*

A hamburger-deficient diet during my childhood in Transylvania must have stunted my growth. Eighty-five billion burgers sold divided by 250 million Americans equals 340 burgers per American. . . . That works out to four extra inches per American over your average Romanian.

CHUCK: *We used to talk about hamburgers in terms of if we stack them all up it would be a stack that would reach the moon and back sixteen times. But I think we have gone quite a way beyond that. So we haven't related it to any more of the planets lately.*

As Chuck and AC converse, Ray Kroc's voice is heard from beyond the grave: *Transfer your fears into faith. And you will inherit the freedom of the future. And if you believe in it—and you believe in it hard—it is impossible to fail.*

And now there is the McLean Deluxe, a skinnier version of the Big Mac for the fat-conscious American of the end-of-the-millennium. McDonald's has so penetrated our national consciousness we even have McPoems now, which are poems mass-produced in writing workshops at universities. And McTests, McThoughts, McReactions, McFeelings, and so on.

No meat eater myself, I watch the vast fields of wheat that end up between Mr. Kroc's buns and the immense lowing herds that lay down their lives for Big Mac. I can see too the intense flows of these commodities through the banks and the money markets—the rivers of commerce paralleling the rivers of wheat and meat, like mind and body.

In the novel *The Pit* by Frank Norris, a madman tries to corner the wheat market. Like Napoleon he is filled with dreams of glory. Every loaf of bread on earth will be stamped with his name. Alas! The drought he prays for does not come. Instead, there is a plentiful harvest. The earth, which rarely sympathizes with the dreams of Napoleons, buries him in wheat. All his plans go awry. The peasants of Europe are starving, and the wheat he has been hoarding spills over the shores of America and feeds them. The Midwest harbors such dreams occasionally. It must be the immensity of her plains that allows imperial daydreams to roll unimpeded.

With Yosi in the Pit

THE PIT where Frank Norris's madman operated from is still thriving. After reading that book, I always wanted to come here to the heart of midwestern trade to watch its mysterious workings. I am lucky. I meet one of the most successful traders of today.

Yosi Morik, an Israeli immigrant, came to the U.S. in 1974 with $70 in his pocket. He drove a cab, was a porter, and went to school at night. This morning, before I had my coffee, he made half a million dollars. He trades exclusively for himself for six months of the year, and sails for the next. In just two days Yosi trades over $100 billion, more than the gross national product of Romania.

YOSI: *I'm so good sometimes it's amazing. It did not come to me the easy way.*

AC: *You think that because you are an Israeli you have a better understanding of capitalism?*

YOSI: *Naw, I have a better understanding of hard work and taking risks. When you are surrounded by tanks in the Golan Heights and there is no way out, you come to this market it looks very easy. I would say safely that in one week I go through a million dollars, but I still drive twenty minutes to a dry cleaner's that does a shirt for $.79 instead of $1.29 because then it's real money, right, but here you trade.*

AC: *It looks like a religious revival meeting, everybody shouting and throwing their hands into the air. If it's a meeting what are they worshiping here?*

YOSI: *They are worshiping their ego first, money second.*

After showing me his big computers through which flow rivers of information from all over the world, Yosi pointed to two places in his chest and told me, "When I feel it here, I sell. When here, I buy. The computers are good . . . but the truth is in my chest."

THE conviction grows in me that Americans, no matter what they do, are animated by hope, not by reason—that a profound intuitive, even mystical, faith underlies all our acts.

"Hear me, O Board, who giveth and taketh!"

Holy Rollers

THE spirit resides equally in roller skates and money pits. I went to a Roller Skating Gospel Rink outside Chicago. On weekend nights hundreds of young black Christians praise the Lord on skates.

I wondered if the capitalist spirit that animated Josi and the do-good-get-the-young-off-the-streets and let-them-vent-into-the-arms-of-the-Lord spirit, are they the same?

ROLLER: *Dear heavenly father, we thank you for this day, we thank you for yet waking us up on this morning. Lord, there is so much that we can thank you for we just cannot tell it all but the devil tries to come in like a flood but we know that you will raise up a standard against him. Amen. Let's give God a praise.*

MUSIC: "Things are getting better all the time"

ROLLER 2: *We are trying to show Christians that there is more to Christianity than just the four walls of the church.*

ROLLER 3: *Christians need a vent also, and rather than a violent vent, why not vent in worship and roller skating. I guess they call us holy rollers.*

I tried putting on skates to get in the rink with Jesus, but all the urgings of the good-hearted rink master couldn't convince me. I felt a most peculiar sensation in my wrist—right at the place where it was going to snap. Mark Roy, our soundman, showed me a scar from roller skating on his wrist, at exactly the place where I was feeling the warning pain. It didn't heal properly and it broke again. They had to take a piece of bone from his hip to fix it. I had broken my share of ankles and wrists, so I decided to forgo it. But what amazing skill and enthusiasm the skating believers showed!

When I look into the round and happy faces of the rollers I see nothing of their lives outside the rink. I cannot tell if they are poor or sick or alone. They are animated by a spirit that is utterly different from that of Karen and Tyree, who also burn bright with spirit. While Karen and Tyree have kept their anger and have sharpened the details

These members of Chicago's roller skating church are praying just before skating. They are letting Jesus know what's in their hearts just before showing Him what they can do with their bodies.

of their lives so that everyone could see them, these skaters have shed their circumstances like old skins. I close my eyes and empathize.

Joy is the grease in my skates, O Lord! And if we skate fast enough and well enough we'll be saved from poverty, from the police, from racism, and from the unsavory details of our own lives! Amen!

Themis of Glencoe

EVERY day in America, the individual spirit clashes with community standards . . . and those appointed to uphold them. Themis Klotz of the wealthy Chicago suburb of Glencoe has buried a car in her front yard and called it Art. Some of her neighbors and the city of Glencoe thought it was garbage. Arguing in court for garbage was Peter Cummins, Glencoe city manager, who is young enough to be Themis's son.

PETER: *When you talk to her, you'll find that she's very much supportive of efforts to stop nuclear waste, nuclear war, other concerns. Why then does she create such a hazard and a problem for her own neighbors?*

THEMIS: *Now, actually I think my neighbors would really be offended if I told them that this is meant to be seen up there by our satellites. . . .*

PETER: *I take no personal joy in pursuing this. We really work hard to respect the individual rights, but I don't want anyone who works for me or I don't want to have to go and explain to a parent that your child has been injured on this property.*

THEMIS: *There's nothing dangerous here, despite allegations to the—*

AC: *Well, we heard it scares the children.*

THEMIS: *Scares them! Look at what they watch on television! This scares them? C'mon.*

PETER: *We actually permit artwork in the front yard, sculptures that have an animal or personlike similarity.*

THEMIS: *This is going to be a mutant dolphin. The car won't be seen when I finish shoveling this pile of sand over there, and then the dolphin shape will be perhaps more evident.*

AC: *So, what are you arguing in court?*

Themis Klotz of Glencoe, Illinois, after the city buried her artwork and left a newspaper over the grave. She is thinking of new ways to unsettle the pinched soul of suburbia.

THEMIS: *First amendment, I hope.*

PETER: *Our argument has nothing to do with speech. That may be her defense, but the village has a very simple case based on these are the laws, you're choosing to violate those laws. What was it the Supreme Court talked about, I'll know pornography when I see it? I know junk when I see it. I know garbage when I see it. And so it's existed for eleven years, because it takes a lot to go after someone like this.*

AC: *Themis was telling me all about the artistic significance of the piece, and a little earlier on, you said that there's a fine difference there between art and trash.*

PETER: *Well, I would agree. I mean that . . . I mean I don't . . .*

THEMIS: *You said that?*

PETER: *You mean is there a fine difference between art and trash, a fine line? Yes, I think there is.*

THEMIS: *Well, I find most people use terms like "trash" and "rubbish" and "garbage" indiscriminately. Y'know, I have not trespassed on nuclear silos in North Dakota, I haven't poured blood, hammered on missiles. I haven't done those things. I'm just gonna do it right here.*

PETER: *How are you not contributing to the problem with this demonstration on this property . . . this junk?*

THEMIS: *Property! Hey!*

PETER: *This is your property.*

THEMIS: *You know, to you it's property. To me, it's home. OK, and I make that distinction with you constantly, because you seem to have a wheeler-dealer mentality that I don't share. You always talk, "deal . . . deal . . . deal." I don't deal.*

PETER: *Well, let's resolve this to somebody's mutual satisfaction.*

THEMIS: *The artist does not allow the integrity of the piece to be vandalized.*

Leaning out of Peter's hearing, Themis says to me: "I didn't even get into the spiritual and religious aspects of my work."

"You don't have to, Themis," I reassured her. "Everybody knows junk art is spiritual in America."

AC: *What is the name of your piece, Themis?*

THEMIS: *Oh, it's the monument to humanity that nobody's gonna be left to build after George Bush has his limited protracted winnable nuclear war with twenty million Americans acceptable losses.*

A Cook County jury ruled in favor of pure junk, however, and forced Themis to bring her lawn in line with standard suburban aesthetics. Here is Themis now, lounging over what used to be "Monument to Humanity No One Will Be Left Behind to Build After George Bush Has His Winnable Protracted Nuclear War with Twenty Million Americans Acceptable Losses."

Westward Bound

Space is the central fact of man in North America.

Charles Olson

THE argument between Klotz and Cummins may be what drove Americans West in search of room to rant and rave. Room to raise up art or garbage. Let's investigate the following road phenomena: is it art or is it garbage? Working definitions: If it leaves behind nothing that will cause animals to choke to death, or humans to die a slow, lingering death, it's art. If not, it's garbage. Seeing God in a rocky butte out of your car window is art. The exhaust from your God-viewing contraption, however, is garbage. Rocky Flats is art. Rocky Flats Nuclear is garbage.

WE drove West to Colorado, toward Denver. I noted the opening of the vistas, the shape of clouds, the presence of large animals, the growing height of humans, and the appearance of hats. Hats keep the sky out of one's hair. The sky is the indisputable boss here: all things grow toward it, sprawl under it, or try to emulate it. Houses are painted sky-blue, the roadside signs are pastel-colored. Whitish-blue animals graze on pale green hills. Even drunks on the street corners of small Colorado towns are wrapped in sky-colored blankets. People talk in short sentences that are like tufts of grass. They open their mouths wide and let the vowels sprawl like small mountain lakes. Nobody looks afraid to breathe. My red Caddy, which looked longer than an ancient lizard in the cramped cities of the East, looks normal here. A rancher who is putting gas in his oversized Ford and twirling a huge cigar between his foot-long digits offers to buy it. "I can use one of those for my kid. She's turning fifteen." I tell him it's not for sale, and inquire whether he wouldn't rather present his baby with something daintier. "Hell, no," he says. "She's been riding horses bigger than this Caddy since she was two." Yep, I think. Mark Twain knew these folk when he said that "their tales are as big as their bellies."

Ivan, New Westerner

MY friend Ivan Suvanjieff, publisher of the excellent literary review *The New Censorship*, was waiting to give me a real look at the West. Ivan moved to Denver drawn in part by the romance of Neal Cassady, who was born by the railroad tracks to a hobo father in the days of depression America. Ivan is from Detroit and he is nostalgic for the common workingman, a now-vanished creature that flourished in the words of Eugene Debs, suffered in the songs of Woody Guthrie, and became at last, in the forties, Neal Cassady's underclass. Neal talked and even wrote something about it but it was Kerouac, who came from another vanishing working-class world in Lowell, Massachusetts, who made it romantic. Ivan is pretty romantic himself. He once lit his cigarette from the Olympic Torch as it swept past him in Detroit, Michigan. Then he had to leave town.

Real Cash Cows

IVAN'S loft, where he makes large spacious paintings, is right behind Neal's dad's railroad tracks. The Denver Rodeo and Stock Show is behind the railroad tracks. The rugged cowboys and the open range have come indoors for business. We go visit.

At the Denver Rodeo & Stock Show I met Gene Weise, a cowboy-hatted millionaire whose company is a leading manufacturer of cows and horses. Gene's products are packages of carefully engineered genetic meat, stirpicultured products of science. The U.S. leads the way in artificial inseminations. Gene ships embryos all over the world. And bull semen, a substance more expensive than illegal drugs. Three "straws" of the stuff cost $150.

While we talked, cowboy businessmen walked by, gambling on their bulls' libidos. I was handed slick brochures with *Playboy*-like centerfolds of bovines: "Ding Ding 21N 2S" (it sounds like a British zip code) is "thick quartered, high maternal influence, goggle-eyed, dark red scrotum, dark red in color, high libido and fertility. . . ." The answer to my dreams! Then there is Crystal, "undoubtedly the greatest cow ever bred at John E. Rice and Sons, Inc." But the greatest is Cossack, another Weise creation, "his abundance of great maternal influence fused with a thick, powerful phenotype, pigmentation, and red meat, will produce the great ones for the cattle breeder seeking proven, consistent genetics."

GENE: *This bull 0237 was the result of artificial insemination. We probably do a better job of selecting in the cattle business than we do in the human race, because we're so very very careful. So we can manage that in the livestock business, but I'm not sure we want to do that too much in the human race.*

AC: *So you believe in love but it doesn't work the same way with cows.*

GENE: *I do believe in love, and it doesn't necessarily work that way with cows.*

AC: *What happens if a bull is attracted to a certain cow, do you keep them apart?*

GENE: *He's a good bull. Look at him chew that cud. Wonderful-headed bull. Isn't that an attractive head for a bull, if you know what I'm talking about . . . ?*

AC: *No, I don't.*

GENE: *These are our new models. We're displaying the 1992 best Hereford female. What makes for fashion? Quality, balance, symmetry, beauty, neckline, beauty of head, refinement, and yet quality throughout. And so femininity in livestock is . . . you can see it, you can observe it, and it's there.*

AC: *Well, I've never been to a Miss America contest. This is the closest I've come.*

GENE: *Well, you're seeing it at its best, maybe, right now. The judge is going to . . . he's sorted these cattle all day, he's made his choices for his division champions, and he's the one who's going to determine which—in his opinion—is the ideal female for the Hereford breed.*

Gene's cows swept the contest. And all their beauty and femininity is going to increase their McDonaldability as they stream into your mouths, meat eaters of America.

I didn't tell Gene that I'm a vegetarian. He might have shot me.

I buy a Universal Semen Sales Hat. I decide against purchasing Sammy Semen's Classic T-Shirt, Semen Running Shorts, Semen Beach Towel, and the Classic Semen Mug.

Gene's pampered inventions have air-conditioned stalls with running water and more amenities than most people in Detroit.

But all is not well among the animals of the West. Wild, starving, abandoned horses are roaming the high plateaus and the deserts. Colorado Horse Rescue finds wild or abandoned horses and places them with families. This nonprofit organization, started by Sharon and Steve Jackson (P.O. Box 1510, Arvada, CO 80001) has rescued hundreds of horses, among them: "Sweet Pea, a 34-inch-high black Shetland trained to drive was abandoned when her owner moved. She was found sleeping on the porch of the empty house, curled up like a big dog. A veterinary student who was looking for a driving pony is her new owner." "Lucky, a Palomino gelding was one of only four survivors of an accident involving an overturned trailer in which forty other horses, all bound for slaughter, were killed. He is now placed with a family who adopted a four-year-old unwanted girl who spent her young life in a series of foster homes."

"Now if someone would adopt lost cowboys like that, everything would be hunky-dory!" Clint Corey told me. Clint is no lost cowboy himself. The reigning world-champion bareback rider, he makes about $100,000 a year, money he invests in his house, his horses, and his "little girl." The bad part is that he's never home. The rodeo circuit

Gene Weise, the emperor of bull semen. Gene creates new
breeds of cattle in his genetic laboratories.

keeps him on the road months at a time. He spends sad evenings in
smoky bars with stuffed heads on the wall, listening to country singers
wail about being all dressed up with no place to go.

High-tech semen, kindness to horses, and lonely cowboys are the
New West. The Old West is another story, and people are touchy about
it. The sculptor Red Grooms made a funny sculpture of settlers and
Indians shooting each other up with wooden bullets and arrows, but
this cartoon vision of the Hollywoodized West so frightened the good
citizens of Denver they had to hide it in the back of the Denver Art
Museum.

The Whites of Their Eyes

THE Western trail is a gunpowder trail. Before they gunned their cars in this direction, white men *shot* their way West. In Romania guns were strictly forbidden. I got years of pleasure out of a wooden gun my stepfather made me. When it broke I cried for days, and was inconsolable until I fell in love.

My girlfriend had a gun. Just kidding.

My father *did* have a gun, though, and it went with his black Packard and his leather jacket. The first of my dreams that I remember featured a truck full of soldiers going by fast. One of them took aim at me with his pistol and shot me dead. I died. I woke up.

I couldn't believe it when I came to the U.S. that you could just go into a store and buy a gun. In Detroit you had to wait three days to buy a revolver but you could always go to Toledo, Ohio, and buy one in two minutes. Then you could go back to Detroit and use it at home.

The lazy proximity of death in America amazed me so much that I wrote a book of poems called *License to Carry a Gun.*

> there is an orange rotting on the table
> closer to freedom than i ever was.
> i'll throw it away soon, its smell
> gives me the same hallucinations
> i had when i was holding a gun.
> orange of sun, my useless state of mind

The speaker in this poem is an imprisoned Puerto Rican poet I had invented in order to explain the violence of America to myself.

After the book was published I went to a little gun-and-grocery shop in Toledo to buy a Coke, and there, on a skimpy book rack, along with *The Shooter's Bible* and *Gun Digest* was my book, *License to Carry a Gun.* "How is it selling?" I asked the clerk. "Fine," he said. OK. It's a bit technical, it's poetry, but what the heck. Most gun owners aren't picky. Richard Brautigan's *Trout Fishing in America* sold to thousands of fishermen before they figured out that the fish in the book were literary.

Once I was arrested in New York for playing with a very realistic wooden gun that my friend and Eighth Street Bookstore co-clerk Dudley made to console me for the loss of my first wooden gun. Dudley is a fine wood sculptor, so the toy he made me was not just realistic, it was scary—it had that extra touch.

I used it to mock-shoot one of my favorite poets, Kenneth Koch, at a poetry reading at St. Mark's Church in New York. Kenneth didn't do anything wrong but I believed back then that one must perform Dada acts on one's elders in order to keep them honest. I don't think Kenneth was thrilled by the sight of a hairy youth pointing a pistol at him and shouting, "Death to bourgeois poetry!" He told me later that he wasn't thrilled at all, but scared. He didn't sound scared at the time, because right after I ran off the stage with my anarchist tresses flailing behind me, he said warily: "Aw, grow up!" It was a *bon mot* under the circumstances. Being a poet I would have preferred that he had uttered something like, "Cherchez la femme!" or "Je haïe le mouvement qui déplace les lignes!," but heck, only Mao thought flowers came out of guns, and he *wrote* that somewhere.

After I "shot" Kenneth I wandered exhilarated into the throbbing evening fauna of Second Avenue, where people of my generation did what they could to entertain each other with glimpses of flesh and eternity. By Gem Spa, the newsstand on the corner of Second and St. Mark's Place, dope dealers, tourists, preteen runaways with sleeping bags, undercover cops, and recently enlightened preachers made a din like a neon beehive. I passed them bouncily, pulling the gun in and out of my pocket without thinking about it. And without thinking about it, two plainclothes cops busted me. "We saw you rob a liquor store, punk!" one of them said. "I did not. I just came from shooting a poet!" I protested vehemently. Good answer. I spent the night at the Tombs, at 100 Centre Street. A killer tried to engage me in sex all night. "Never again," I told myself, "never again will you play with guns!"

I know only too well that these beastly things kill without rhyme or reason and that we are all victims of it. Call it irrational boyish fascination, the immature nostalgia of a reader of Westerns (I was on a Louis L'Amour kick for a whole month), but I'm still not listening to myself. I'm in thrall to these shiny toys of death.

I HEAR that one of my compatriots is shooting around here. The Caddy climbs the mountain road toward Colorado Springs, where he dwells. I watch the hills and plains of America disappear below me. The air is cold and crisp and, it seems to me, something sober and sharp has entered the air.

Dan and His Daughters

DAN IUGA, once the gold medalist for Romania, is training the U.S. Olympic Shooting Team. He teaches me how to shoot. We are shooting .38-caliber bullets. He straightens my shoulders, corrects my posture, points me in the right direction, and tells me to squeeze the trigger gently. I do, but I'm nearsighted, and have no idea if I hit the target or not. As my bullets whiz through the air, Iuga tells me that he cries every time he hears the U.S. national anthem at the Olympics. In Romania, he says, he didn't feel anything when the Romanian anthem was played. "There was something false about that anthem," he says thoughtfully, furrowing his brow as if engaged in deep philosophical speculation. "But the American—" he brightens up and puts a hand over his heart.

Dan has trained some of America's best young shooters, and he loves guns. He's also a licensed gun dealer and a member of the NRA, which accounts for part of his enthusiasm. The other part is that, like most Romanians (not me), he's a ham. A ham with a gun.

Dan has done his best work with the two American teenagers who are assembling their specially constructed guns next to us. Laura and Yolana, his daughters, are both National Pistol Shooting Champions on the Junior Olympics team. Yolana is popping gum as she loads up.

They are both blue-jeaned floppy-shirted American teenagers who love the mall. Laura tells me that for the longest time she didn't like country music but lately she's been getting into it. Still, rock 'n' roll is Yolana's favorite music. But shopping, well, that's *deevine*. . . . They both have just a bit of Romanian accent as they let go, boom, boom, boom, and hit every target dead center!

Dan Iuga, coach of the U.S. Olympic pistol-shooting team, with daughters Laura and Yolana, junior Olympians. The Iugas are originally from Romania. Here, they take aim at communism, flag-burners, and liberals. (Eric Paddock)

Daddy is very proud. His office is full of trophies, his daughters can shoot better than Jesse James, the flag waves in the breeze, guns sell briskly, Americans fall down dead . . . boom . . . boom . . . boom . . . millions of us killed by guns every day. I put my best liberal foot forward and say to the girls, "Guns don't produce painless TV death. They kill real people. Do you think there is glamour in death?" They both rise indignantly in defense of their daddy's livelihood. "Guns guarantee freedom. In Romania, there would have never been a Ceauşescu if everyone had a gun." Right.

"The right to bear arms . . ." We bear them and *bear* them. They are our cross. Stand up, salute, and writhe in pain. The march of death begins each morning in the land of the brave and the free. There are guns in the hands of children in the cities. I look into Laura and Yolana's nearly innocent faces bursting with youth, delight, and energy, and want to say, Go shopping! Leave those guns at home! On the other hand, aggression and violence are always the privileged domain of youth and enthusiasm.

The girls remind me of some of my LSU students, bursting with health and right-wing rhetoric, their well-trained bodies just waiting for *something* . . . an order to march, an urge to scream, an itch to shoot.

I taught a morning class last year and we had a discussion about guns. One of my students was an eighteen-year-old freshman who always looked impeccably dressed and carefully made up by 8 A.M., a feat few of her classmates could rival. Most of them looked as if they'd just tumbled out of some hayloft and put on whatever was handy: a man's shirt, a milkman's overalls, a clown's suspenders. After listening for a while to various opinions on guns, my perfect belle said that she always carried a gun. She opened her school bag and drew out a two-barreled Derringer pistol. Her initials were engraved in gold on the pearl handle.

"Who gave it to you?"

"My daddy," she said.

I asked her if she'd ever had occasion to use it.

"Well, yes," she said. "I had a date in New Orleans and got a flat on the Causeway. I was standing there and this man stopped. He was a bad man. He said he didn't have time to change my tire but that he'd drive me to a phone. Right. So I took this out . . ." She patted her gun with a tender hand. ". . . pointed it at him, and said, 'Change that tire!' And you know what? He *did!*"

The class collapsed laughing but they weren't laughing *at* her, they were laughing *with* her. They all approved of my perfect magnolia. A true southern belle. Made of sugar and steel.

An excess of well-being always leads to fascism. I was mildly glad that they were all happy, well fed, alive, enthusiastic, and . . . armed. But I prefer the depressed, wan youth of the inner cities, dressed in black and not so sure about the greatness of America.

Firing with Bo

DAN and his daughters are the sunny side of the American dream. Sport, and "My Country 'Tis of Thee." Between the sunny side and the West Los Angeles underside, there are other sides. One of these sides is in full symbolic bloom at the Survival Store in Las Vegas. The Survival Store billboard ad towers over a wide boulevard, featuring Bo, all-American girl in tiny bikini with large machine gun between well-turned legs. Bo's real-life beau is Chuck, who runs the Survival Store with a handful of unemployed mercenaries.

Bo is the grownup version of Laura and Yolana. She has wedded Eros and Death, the chief drives of advertising, in the raw.

BO: *Well, I've been in* Penthouse *and* Playboy. *When I was little, not only did my dad get me into weapons, but my mom always had a photographer take pictures of me every year. To be an American, in America, owning machine guns is the best thing in the world.*

AC: *Tell me what it feels like to shoot a gun.*

BO: *Exhilarating. Especially a machine gun. It's something that nobody does, that people think is taboo, so you're out there doing something that nobody else is doing and you just feel exhilarated.*

Now let me see your position. All right. Put it against your shoulder, keep your finger off the trigger until you are ready to fire the weapon. Now lean forward . . .

Bo teaches Japanese tourists and deprived immigrants like me to unload big guns into the western mountains.

BO: *Now you want to hold it on this shoulder, right there, and kind of lean forward with the top of your body . . . that's good. All right right now rock and roll, pull the trigger all the way back and let it go. Great!*

AC: *So, Bo, how did you get into this?*

BO: *My dad gave me a handgun when I was five years old.*

AC: *Why did your daddy give you a gun when you were five?*

BO: *Why did he give it to me? He wanted me to know about handguns, and he wanted me to become strong.*

Bo's strong. And nice. Everybody in America is nice. And crazy. It's a nice and crazy thrill to ride in a bumpy weapons carrier with Bo on a beautiful desert morning. The wind blows her hair over her eyes, the sky is vast, blue, and indifferent.

Bo teaches shooting for three different fees in three different garbs: dressed in fatigues, sexy, and nude. When we arrived in the desert, there was a discussion as to which garb or nongarb was best for our movie. Roger, ever mindful of PBS, argued for fatigues. Jean, the

Bo, my shooting instructor, instructing me on the proper way to shoot a machine gun.

cameraman, argued for sexy—a black brassiere over short fatigue shorts. I argued for nude. The brisk, chilly breeze that blew from the mountains at Chuck's ranch did not bother Bo, daughter of the wild and of nude modeling.

While we discussed the issue, the fatigue-clad men setting up our toys complained that there was little work these days. Peace was breaking out all over the place . . . there were fewer and fewer want ads in *Soldier of Fortune* magazine . . . setting up heavy-caliber machine guns for weapon-starved Japanese (and a Romanian now and then) wasn't exactly high-paying work. Cambodia, now that was good money. . . .

In the end, Roger had his way, as he always seemed to. Bo kept her military drag on. Dan Klein, Roger's assistant, advanced the idea of some possibly sexist interpretation of this entire episode. Well, of course, I said, but it's not *our* sexism. I wanted Bo to teach me naked.

Like Dan Iuga she adjusted my posture, straightened me out, and put my finger on the trigger. I squeezed it and fired several bursts at bowling pins set at various intervals on the hill. Rock 'n' roll! I missed them all!

I had expressly requested from Roger that I shoot either at cars or at TV sets. No. PBS. Too poor for cars, too ambiguous for TV. OK. After several rounds of this, I became dissatisfied. It was . . . too easy. I was also a terrible shot. Roger, who had declared his hatred for guns and who had never fired one, picked up the machine gun at Bo's urging, and with barely any lessons . . . boom . . . boom . . . knocked out all the bowling pins. Bo grinned.

Chuck then set up a huge World War I machine gun with a bullet belt for me. I lay on my stomach and fired off some huge shells. Man-sized chunks of dirt were ripped out of the flesh of the hill where my ammo hit. All I needed was a bigger gun and a bigger target!

While I tore the shit out of the Nevada landscape,* Chuck told me that survival was about self-sufficiency, about needing nothing but a gun and a Bo and maybe a mule. I asked him if he believed in Armageddon. I told him that I had heard that survivalists all over the West were laying in supplies for the final confrontation with liberals, Jews, blacks, feminists, homosexuals, pro-choicers, and vegetarians. Chuck dodged these questions, which he wasn't about to answer on

---

*A national pastime, see A bombs.

camera. He declared himself a simple American patriot like John Wayne. "When *it* comes," he said, "we'll be ready." I asked him what "it" was but he gazed absentmindedly at the Nevada hill I'd been pumping full of bullets. I had the distinct feeling that *I* was *it*.

Driving away from the Survival Store, Roger said, "I never felt more like a Jew in my whole life." Yeah. And he can shoot.

THE contradictory impulses of the American spirit flourish here in the West: shooting and transcending. We shoot our way across the land while simultaneously raising our arms to the sky and trying to be better and bigger than we are.

And then there is Bo, urging us on like Delacroix's Liberty to shoot and transcend some more.

Shooting Back

WESTERNERS take their guns seriously. So do Native Americans. Their history is one of genocide on an unimaginable scale. My thirteen-year-old son, Tristan, tells me that he had a dream that he went back into the past and gave guns to all the Indians. "What happened then?" I ask. "I don't know," he says. "I woke up." That's right. The national nightmare went on for a long time. It's still going on. We haven't woken up yet, but we are too far along in the bad dream to go back and change the beginning.

"The earth is an Indian thing!" It was, and it is. The farther west I travel, the stronger the *genii loci*, the spirits of place. Here, it is the land that shapes the minds of those who live on it.

Taos Pueblo

THE Taos Pueblo is one of the oldest inhabited villages in North America. It is a commune. The center of the village has bread-baking ovens and adobe houses. The poles of the kivas where the secret ceremonies take place poke out of the ground. The pueblo ceremonies have remained secret here, although similar rituals have been described by anthropologists, to the distress of Native Americans. There is an uneasy truce between Anglos, Chicanos, and Native Americans here. The hippies, with their idealistic enthusiasm for Indian ways, have adopted some of the rituals. There is a sweat lodge near Taos where a mixed group of New Mexicans practice the peyote ritual. I found out to my astonishment that the peyote drummer of this lodge is a crazy Lower East Side anarchist I knew in the sixties. Tonio, a wiry Italian from the lineage of Sacco and Vanzetti, used to start riots on summer nights on the Lower East Side. I remember him speaking frenziedly to idle mobs on St. Mark's Place, urging them to overturn police cars. Which they often did, turning the Village into a madhouse of sirens, ambulances, and embattled streets. I am not surprised that he is a drummer now (the drum keeps the peyote dreamers on course through the myriad experiences of the trip), but I would have thought that the FBI, which looked for him for years, would have caught up with him by now. Not only is he a drummer but he has mapped an underground horse trail through deserts and mountains for radicals evading the law.

AT the Taos Pueblo, I met two young Taos artists active in community life. Robert Mirabel is building a house in the middle of Taos village. After some wandering in the outside, he has returned to the oldest traditions of his tribe. He tells me that those who let their minds be shaped by the land must fight those for whom the land is only to be used, exploited, left devastated and abandoned. The Taos Pueblo is not among the worst-exploited Native American tribes in the West—they have land, the young still respect the traditions—and yet here too, like elsewhere on Turtle Island, as Natives call America, blows the desolate wind of loss, alienation, sorrow, and regret for an order that is forever gone. . . .

ROBERT: *This is Taos Pueblo—where we are called the red willow people. This is not, definitely not, America. I don't consider it America.*

AC: *How does this community survive within this larger and different world?*

ROBERT: *Well, you know money runs everything, that's what America wants, you can't go out and wear skins and go out and hunt with bow-and-arrows elk or deer. That life is gone. Always in America, they say how far can I get, how far can I succeed—who do I have to punch down—who do I have to step on to get to what I want. Right here it is not that. It's the unity, the community helps the earth.*

Robert's friend Benito Concha is a dancer and a peace activist who has traveled all over the world. Benito's father and grandfather were tribal governors. His grandmother, a wonderfully ancient and wrinkled wise woman, keeps watch over three generations from the adobe roof of her little house. Inside are two granddaughters nursing their babies. On the walls are portraits of her sons meeting important people. Traditional Indian bundles of corn hang from the ceiling. A toddler plays with a kachina doll.

Benito is very proud of his grandma. He hugs her and tells her in Tewa, the Pueblo language, that we are here to make a movie. He is going to dance for us.

BENITO: *She always lived inside the pueblo all her life, doesn't know a house or home anywhere else but inside this pueblo.*

When we dance, we dance with the earth. The willow hoop is fragile once brought into a circle. Eventually if you just mess around with nature, the hoop will be broken, and that is what this dance represents.

We don't do these dances like for a sort of Mickey Mouse Club type of thing. Each song and dance is a prayer to show the people out here that we are trying to keep our ways. And it's hard to live in two worlds.

As Benito dances, there seems to be just one world. But as tourists gather to gawk, and start taking pictures, it's evident that another is right there.

The Native American spirit, this continent's most finely tuned spirituality, is, paradoxically, not provincial at all. Benito, traditional Taos Pueblo dancer and jeweler, also plays in a rock 'n' roll band. While he takes off his traditional dress, we talk about William Burroughs, the writer whose vision of nightmare earth is equally relevant to the young uprooted punks of the Lower East Side of New York. Buffaloes graze outside, on a mountain pasture that became Taos land by a presidential act of Richard M. Nixon. A revered portrait of Nixon hangs in the village church.

Peter Rabbit

I WAS introduced to Roberto and Benito by my friend Peter Rabbit, who teaches in the Pueblo school. In the sixties, Peter was the founder of the Libre commune, which was a village of geodesic domes made from cannibalized car bodies. It was inhabited by a tribe of visionary hippies who wanted to be Indians and used peyote to commune with the land. Peter now runs in Taos the World Heavyweight Poetry Championship, a summer solstice event that brings the town to a fever pitch of gambling and poetic speculation. The bout consists of ten rounds. Each round consists of one poem, and the last round is improvisational: the poets pick their subject out of a hat. I was World Heavyweight Poetry Champion in 1987, when I beat Lewis McAdams in front of the entire town of Taos, cheering, booing, and taking loud bets after each round. The mayor of Taos handed me the Max, a heavy cast-iron sculpture named after New Mexico's beloved poet Max Finstein. It set off every alarm at the airport. Some of the past heavyweights include Anne Waldman, Ntozake Shange, Gregory Corso, Victor Hernandez Cruz, Al Simmons.

Here are Peter Rabbit and Al Simmons, after an exhibition match. Since this wasn't an official bout, they are both smiling happily. In past years, losers have been known to throw themselves into the Rio Grande, which is particularly ferocious in this area. The winners go to the hot springs at Ojo Caliente instead and sit in caves full of mineral steam.

Peter was shot last Christmas by a Pueblo boy looking for a deer to bring to a Taos initiation ceremony. Peter had just cut a small Christmas tree and was asking forgiveness of the forest gods when the shots rang out. The Indian boy carried him over his shoulder just like a deer and drove him to the hospital. Several complicated operations later, Peter is back in business. He will be able to walk without crutches in a few months. Ironically, the boy had been one of his students from the Pueblo where Peter teaches poetry.

Peter's wife, Annie, is a poet. Theirs is one of those houses that make America home for me. Surrounded by an ocotillo fence, the little adobe house squats like a tiny animal under the huge stars of the New Mexican sky. It is a center of the poetry universe. I sat here many late nights with poets from all over the United States talking the world out of harming us. Peter's grin always made people want to get up and dance. Which is precisely what Peter will do when he's off his crutches.

Al Simmons and Peter Rabbit after a grueling match of wits at the World Heavyweight Poetry Championship in Taos, New Mexico.

Holy Dirt

Chimayo

THE old ways of the Pueblo and speed-driven America are not the only worlds here. The Spanish conquistadors taking the land in the name of the Holy Faith—Santa Fe—have also been here and put their iron stamp on everything. But, in the end, the Indian earth has infused the Catholic faith with its magic. Indian and Spanish gods still mingle explosively.

In 1813 Don Bernardo Abeyta, a self-flagellating *penitente*, found a crucifix buried here. He removed it three times, but each time it returned miraculously to the ground where the Santuario de Chimayo now stands. Ever since, a long procession of the sick, the weary, the afflicted, and the crippled have made their way to the Santuario to rub holy dirt on their wounded flesh. The Santuario is surrounded by shrines of the Tewa Indians of the Rio Grande, which are built on the mesas, hills, and mountains. According to Indian beliefs, the mesas, hills, and mountains are themselves sacred spots. Looking over the undulating landscape, with its bright and intense colors, I can feel their power. Numerous Indian legends speak of curative mud in this spot. Santo Niño de Atocha, a Holy Infant, sits in the Santuario wearing little shoes and a basket. It is said that at night Santo Niño walks about healing the sick. He wears out his shoes walking so people bring baby shoes to leave at the shrine.

Three hundred thousand pilgrims come to Chimayo every year. There are so many some of them get killed by traffic. I spoke to some

Holy chatchkas at the Santuario de Chimayo, New Mexico.

of them inside the tiny church, beside the hole containing the miraculous sand.

PILGRIM 1: *This is the Holy Dirt.*

AC: *Did you come to the Santuario de Chimayo for yourself?*

PILGRIM 2: *He broke his hip so we brought him down, and I hope he heals fast. We have faith in it. Like all my uncles and aunts that have passed away, they believed in it.*

Prostheses abandoned by those miraculously cured by holy chatchkas at Santuario de Chimayo.

The holy dirt of Chimayo that cures cripples restored my travel-weary heart. I was ready to leave behind my hidden ailments, my regrets, my tics, my anxieties. I rubbed holy dirt on my responsible adult self.

My friend Simone Lazzeri, who lives in Santa Fe, told me that a drunk with a Ph.D. she knew went to Chimayo to get cured. Next day his wife had him hospitalized.

Nonetheless, I feel the burdens lifting, and even our cynical New York movie crew is beginning to feel the cleansing power of the New Mexico earth. We almost forget the nasty octopus of the twentieth century leveling the planet with its machines outside the adobe walls. Blessed be the simple in spirit for they shall briefly forget the freeways and gas stations!

Cave People

THE old gods were worshiped in caves. The Taos pueblo ceremonies are conducted in underground kivas. Sacred shamans dance on the murals of Lascaux and Altamira. In Rome, there was Mithra, god of the Roman legions, to whom bulls were sacrificed. I once imagined an underground women's world through which flowed the river Aurelia.

Cave-god building the new underground in northern New Mexico.

In northern New Mexico, modern cavemen artists are practicing sacred rites. Mark, a painter, started building himself a closet and ended up creating a sacred labyrinth. There are numerous caves behind his house now. When I was visiting, a silent, muscled, godlike man named Rha, whom Mark had hired to help him extend his labyrinth, was making caves with a pickaxe in the bowels of the mountain. He was wearing only a loincloth. I had been warned by Mark that Rha rarely shows himself, but when I began wandering about on my own, he came out briefly because he listens to the radio as he pickaxes his way into the flesh of the mountain, and he had heard me speak and liked it. Rha studied me for a second, grinned, then picked up his pickaxe. The interview was over.

Painters, dancers, musicians, and meditators come here from as far as Germany to work and live in these caves.

Mark is reluctant to dwell on the rather obvious symbolic significance of the place, but his guests are less shy. I discuss with Ulrike Arnold, a German artist who has painted rocks in Australia, the Grand Canyon, and elsewhere, the significance of the landscape. Caves from different times and places connect with each other underground, she tells me. They are the places where conquered people, defeated religions, escaped convicts, and alienated artists have gone to hide and to practice. I tell her that in a sense there is a vast underground under America that we get hints of only now and then. It's a human as well as a geological underground. Ulrike grinds colored stones to make pigment which she then uses, following the natural coloring and contour of rocks and earth. She squats as she works, mashing her pigments, her blond hair falling all over her face like a Neolithic veil.

It's a lovely even temperature inside the womb of Mother Earth.

Friends I Lost to Gurus

WHAT is it about the composition of this soil that makes it so hospitable to religious mystery?

Even ancient Tibetan Buddhism has found a home here. There are two lamas at this New Mexico stupa: Lama Dorge, a Tibetan traditionalist in a male-dominated religion, and Lama Sara Harding, who is American, Jewish, and feminist. We drink strong Tibetan tea while we talk. Lama Harding's daughter joins us in the room, asking breezy American child questions. I fancy for a moment that I can see Lama Harding's aura: burnished gold on the outside, silver ash inside—as if she's burnt all her emotions. Which is clearly not true because there are hints of extreme sentiment in the exchanges with her kid.

She translates from Lama Dorge's Tibetan after warning me that she may not agree with everything he says. After she translates something she doesn't agree with, she makes her own comment, first in English, then in Tibetan for the Lama, who further disagrees, and so on, a translingual tour de force that's almost as moving as the chanting that follows. The two lamas mirror our American society . . . this is not an escapist practice. One is encouraged to become aware of everything in Buddhist meditation. The desired result is clarity. One comes to it, however, after endless detours in a world of illusions. On the Tibetan wheel representing the universe, there are beautiful angels and horrific soul-eating demons. As the wheel turns, one realizes that they are one and the same. I chant along, feeling peace. Or something like it.

MANY of my friends are Buddhists. Does meditating calm them amid the anxious end-of-millennium American life? I love the title of one of Frank O'Hara's poetry books, *Meditations in an Emergency*. It always epitomized for me the best one can do under the circumstances of contemporary American life: shutting one's eyes for a moment while factories close, people hurt, cities burn. . . . But perhaps there is a better, deeper, longer meditation. I can't tell.

Lama Dorge before Tibetan stupa near Santa Fe. The Lama loves to watch his guests drink sweet Tibetan tea made with butter.

I ONCE wrote a book called *Friends I Lost to Gurus.* It was about my God-crazy friends who migrated from one teacher to another in the sixties and the seventies, donning robes and shedding habits, changing diets, languages, and hair styles in search of that indefinable something that's still driving people everywhere and nowhere but always away from wherever they came from, always looking for a family different from the one they were born into. And who can blame them? The American family today consists most likely of a work-crazed mom trying to raise shopping-mall TV brats in a world gone consumption-mad.

The Sikhs

A BLUE-TURBAN-CLAD bodyguard with a pistol on his hip is patrolling the length of a huge black limousine. This is the private bodyguard of the spiritual leader of the Sikhs of the Western World, Siri Singh Sahib Bhai Sahib Harbhajan Singh Khalsa Yogiji, known as Yogi Bhajan. The yogi has just come in from an overnight flight from Asia, and is now resting in the Albuquerque house of one of his followers. Men, women, and children dressed in bright white cloth are swarming about him, tending to his needs. The women are preparing a several-course vegetarian lunch in the kitchen. The presence of our television crew does not upset the Sikhs, who go about their business as if camera crews were a normal occurrence. There are numerous Sikh communities in the United States, and hosting Yogi Bhajan is a great honor.

The yogi has been touring the Pacific East. I asked him if he had traveled in order to make converts and spread the word. He laughed and said, "No, I was traveling in search of business opportunities." He then became serious in the manner of one sharing an important tip: "The best business opportunities today are in the Pacific rim and in Eastern Europe." Being an Eastern European myself, I felt obliged to return the favor, and advised him to invest in Rand McNally. With so many borders changing, and new countries emerging, map making is bound to become a booming business. His followers listened to our conversation carefully, interjecting comments now and then when they felt that their leader might be projecting the wrong image.

Yogi Bhajan's closest advisers seemed to be products of our better East Coast schools, and some of the yogi's worldly wisdom has a distinctly Jewish flavor to it. I wonder if *all* the Eastern gurus who were successful in America have Jewish-flavored wisdom. Many American Sikhs are well-educated Jews and there are Jews in most of America's spiritual movements that had their beginnings in the psychic explosion of the sixties. My friend Stanley served a couple of gurus with whom he became quickly disenchanted, but not before he taught them an amazing number of survival tricks. Certainly, one Jewish word that many of these Eastern saints have fully earned is "chutzpah."

I asked Yogiji if his community was a cult.

YOGI: *Cult? What is a cult?*

SIKH: *Nobody in our community knows what a cult is.*

AC: *A cult is a group that follows a charismatic leader.*

YOGI: *Forget that part, they don't follow anybody. Religiously to survive, we have to have hierarchy and that way I'm Siri Singh Sahib, it means I am almost a pope. That's why I met a pope like a pope.*

AC: *Where and when did you become enlightened?*

YOGI: *I never use those high-frequency words. I feel God made every human by his own choice and everybody's as enlightened as you can be. And holy, I say you have nine holes. If you take care of them, what comes in and gets out, you are holy.*

AC: *This is a very successful and wealthy community, and—*

YOGI: *Poverty is a curse.*

AC: *Yes?*

YOGI: *We don't believe that. You can't be poor. If you are poor, you are stupid. I don't believe anybody should be poor. I don't believe that anybody should be unhappy. Because we are made in the perfect*

*Siri Singh Sahib Bhai Sahib Harbhajan Singh Khalsa Yogiji,
known as Yogi Bajan, spiritual leader of the Sikhs of the
Western World, also my unofficial investment adviser.*

*image of God. Isn't that what you believe? So how can the perfect make
imperfect beings?*

The Khalsa family, Dharm Singh, Guru Kirn, their daughter Hari
Rai, and baby Siri Sahib, are your average, run-of-the-mill American
Sikh family. I sat in their well-appointed living room, which looked for
all practical purposes like a middle-class advertisement for *House*

Beautiful. Sesame Street was on television. Mom Guru Kirn switched channels. Big Bird disappeared.

GURU KIRN to daughter Hari: *Is that better? I thought you didn't want to watch the letters.*

HARI: *I did.*

GURU KIRN: *Do you want to get him back?*

HARI: *Yeah.*

DHARM SINGH, DAD: *Sometimes it's easier to just sit back, turn on the TV, tune out, drink a beer, but we don't do that. Sometimes we get in an argument, believe it or not . . . you know, married couple . . . you know, we get into an argument and what do you do with that energy? If you can remember, honey, let's not argue, we do love each other, let's sit down, breathe together, think about God together, do a mantra, whatever it is at that time. . . .*

GURU KIRN: *. . . to clear the space.*

DHARM SINGH: *. . . to clear the space, clear our heads.*

GURU KIRN: *You know we also try to do the same thing with Hari Rai, y'know, if she starts getting one of these temper tantrums that are so famous, you know, we have a time out. She goes into her room, she knows how to center herself.*

DHARM SINGH: *What we have is a meditation, a spiritual practice, it's the meaning of Sadna—*[to Hari] HEY, QUIET!—*which we do every day without fail, and there's a real power in that. Sometimes it's very difficult, sometimes you just practically sleep through it, other times it's an incredible spiritual moving connection with God, the whole thing.*

The Sikhs are American patriots. There is no Bruderhof-like poverty among them. There is no TV-less atoning here for the sins of capitalism. *Au contraire,* the Sikhs celebrate capitalism, wealth, and might. They sell America the oats for her granola, and operate one of the largest security companies in the state. The extreme bright whiteness of their clothes was the only truly strange element in the upper-

*Sikh Madonna
and child
demonstrating the
sanctity of
babyhood.*

middle-class living room. When I asked Guru Kirn the oft-asked question about how Sikhs keep their whites so white, she replied that she never wears the same outfit twice.

Sikh children go to high school in India, where they receive British public school discipline and no doubt get to experience Somerset Maugham–like heartbreak and sorrow. On this subject I received rather evasive answers from the well-behaved teenagers I spoke to. One of them told me that it was lonely at the beginning. And not so long ago, when the Sikhs were at war with the Hindu community around them, things got scary. They were besieged in their school for a few days. Some of them flew back. In fact, the American Sikhs do not feel very comfortable with the politics of their co-religionists. Yogi Bhajan's moderate positions had incurred the wrath of Sikh extremists, who do not understand America. It's a touchy subject. The heavily armed guard claims that these extremists are one of the reasons why he must be constantly alert.

I accompanied the Khalsas to the temple for the midday prayer and communal lunch. In this beautiful Oriental structure, which is the heart of community life, the Sikhs meet twice a day to pray and to sing. The Sikh ritual is quite beautiful. The songs reverberated through the hall. Indian Sikhs have a long tradition of exalted music and poetry that is almost erotic in its abandon. A delicious communal vegetarian dinner followed the ceremony, and once more we talked.

Sikhs in the don't-mess-with-us mode. They mean it.

SIKH 1: *We may look different. We may practice different, but what we practice is one of the last major religions that was ever formed on this planet. It's very mainstream.*

SIKH 2: *We have a warrior tradition—that we defend righteous-ness—so people don't even come close because they know that we will protect what we have, and we're ready to protect what we have.*

The Sikhs are so reputed for their fierceness that they have been hired by the government to guard military installations. The warrior tradition of the Indian Sikhs has translated well to this country. Their martial values mesh well with the redneck bellicosity of the Western-ers among whom they live. I witnessed an exceedingly graceful sword dance. Men and women receive extensive weapons training, and not just in sword fighting. They have an arsenal of firearms. Because of their religious dress they are not allowed to serve in the U.S. Army, but they have petitioned the government in court for the right to serve wearing turbans.

Not many citizens in the town of Espanola, New Mexico, where they live, care to antagonize the community. There had been some trouble in the past with the Chicano lowriders. Yogi Bhajan told me laughing that they had shot up his house a few times. But he didn't say why or how the hassle stopped. I could only imagine. I would hate to see a serious conflict arise between these Sikhs and the outside world. They would fight until they were all dead.

I am struck again by how white the Sikhs are. Not just their clothes, but their membership.

As I drove through the gates of the Sikh village in Espanola, New Mexico, I felt that somehow I knew all these folks. They were the friends I lost to gurus in the sixties and the seventies, grown a bit older. They had children and opinions just like the rest of us, only they had decided not to live like the rest of us. They made me uneasy. Is there something wrong with the rest of us? Are we not white enough? Not aggressive enough? Not sufficiently God-fearing? Probably—speaking for myself. On the other hand, the oddness of a theocratic hierarchy right in the middle of a representative democracy isn't calculated to make me feel any better.

Lowriders

IN Espanola, the Chicanos who would dare antagonize the Sikhs have a colorful and noisy culture. They make their cars low to the ground, and they turn some of them into shrines as elaborate as Chimayo. They cruise at sunset on the main drag of Espanola, slowing down traffic and driving tourists and cops crazy.

Joe Martinez is one of the elders of lowriding. He formed The Miracles, a lowrider club, after he was run over by a cop in a squad car and lay in a coma for eight days. When he came to, which was a miracle after the injuries he'd suffered, he had a vision of The Miracles Club, and of his Ideal Cholo. His wife put her inheritance at Joe's disposal, and after years of work he made a resplendent automobile shrine that is truly a work of art. His children want to be lowriders. The Miracles take their name seriously; it's a kind of Holy Family, Familia Santa. Joe is the Patriarch of the Heavenly Cholo.

Christ in Espanola, New Mexico, demonstrating humility.

Naturally, there is a great neon Virgin inside the symbolically stuffed and religiously suffused cholo, temple of the Divine Carburetor. Thanks to my sensitivity training among the Buddhists and the Sikhs I can see the shining rays that emanate from Joe like rainbows from a puddle of gasoline. The Gospel According to Joe Martinez. True Chicano culture—LA LUZ DEL CORAZÓN!

And the cop who ran him over? "He shot somebody already in handcuffs," says Joe. "He's still on the force."

Lisa Law, First Hippie

LISA LAW, formerly of the Diggers, was Santa Fe's original hippie. With husband, Tom Law, she was at the intersection of the hippie nomad routes of the sixties. Everyone came to them: Janis Joplin, Taj Majal, Timothy Leary, Bob Dylan, Paul Krassner, Wavy Gravy, Peter Fonda, Dennis Hopper, and countless of the restless spirit seekers of that time, guided by LSD and the utopian imperative to reconnect with Native America. Part of the human underground of that time has now surfaced in the New Age. Another part sank deep below the awareness of modern America. And yet another part has merged with the workaday world of the nineties and become indistinguishable to the naked eye.

In some ways, Yogi Bhajan and the American Sikhs are Lisa Law's creation. In 1968 Yogi was living at her house in Los Angeles. He wanted to take his yoga students to the Renaissance Fair but the fair did not allow longhairs onto the hallowed grounds of the middle class. Lisa had the bright idea to dress them all in white and hide their hair inside turbans. They got in as a religious group, and they stayed that way. It's not an ignominious beginning: the Mormons started with less. In fact, most religions begin rather casually. Lisa was a Sikh for a brief time, but her independent spirit soon clashed with the rigors of community and with the yogi's ego.* While I visited with the community, she waited outside the gates, smoking defiant cigarettes. (Cigarettes, like meat, are strictly forbidden among the Sikhs.)

*Something he claims he doesn't have.

Lisa is standing outside the only still working Hog Farm bus, a legendary vehicle that could tell incredible stories. The Hog Farm, a rolling hippie circus of the sixties, took humor, paradox, street theater, drugs, and sex into deep recesses of rural America, as well as Mexico and Central America. Talking to Lisa is like looking through a kaleidoscope at a kaleidoscopic time that seems like a fairy tale now. One can only dimly imagine the psychic explosion of those days because their complex texture can be translated only tentatively in words and pictures. Lisa, who was everywhere, from Monterey to Woodstock, has brought up a bright sliver of that time in her documentary film *Flashing on the Sixties.*

I have done a bit of prospecting of those days, too, as has anyone who

Lisa Law, First Hippie of Santa Fe, with legendary Hog Farm bus.

was even dimly awake then. But the form that best communicates the mystery is still face-to-face talk, relentless storytelling, laughter.

Lisa now helps drive from the hippie age into the New Age. I am not a great fan of the often sanctimonious and overly specialized language with which New Age practitioners lure their legions of the wounded to the fold. And yet America has experienced such a loss of soul in the past two decades I think that there is nothing wrong with retrieving a little love for yourself from the toxic pits of the postindustrial age.

In nineties America, working for peanuts, or not working at all, or working in a soulless place will steal anyone's soul.

The New Age

LISA: *Why are the hippies into the New Age stuff? Well, you know, we're getting the message directly now from up above. There's no gurus anymore, we're out of the Piscean Age into the Age of Aquarius, and it's funneling down right into the top of our heads, right into our pituitary glands, and it's coming out our heart. And we're going to love everybody!*

The young hippies in Lisa's psychedelic bus are actually cast members in a local revival of *Hair.* For all practical purposes they look— take fifteen or twenty years—like the real thing.

HAIR REVIVAL HIPPIE: *The sixties was a time when everybody really opened up. Everybody reached out, they expressed themselves, but there was a lot of drugs and there was a lot of other things kinda . . . maybe kind of clouding it over, and I think the nineties is the time when we got to get the same feeling but it's gonna be with total awareness and being awake without the drugs.*

OK, if you say so, young hopeful fellow!

The New Age, conservative child of the hippie sixties, is commercially savvy. In Santa Fe, the New Age gets marketed at Ark Books, run by Jamil Kilbride. The day that I visit Ark, the place is an anthology

*Young hippies inside legendary Hog Farm bus in Santa Fe,
singing "This is the Age of Aquarius" with such sincerity,
passersby burst into tears. (Public Policy Productions)*

of New Age psychics, writers, local artists, and assorted hangers on. I think that if I were to disappear even for a moment, there would be a dozen people pointing to exactly the place where I was hiding.

For decades now, Santa Fe's magic pull has lured here an extraordinary array of sensitive people. Until recently, they all had the excuse of art or writing for their practice of magic. But the last wave is unabashedly mystical. You can practically see everyone's third eye.* Jamil hits some chimes as we go from the alchemy room into the Native Magics room.

JAMIL: *A little celestial harmonics on the way in. We're heading into the room that contains the shamanism, Native American, astrology, that side of the family. What really sparks me in my work here is that we can provide for people a spiritual supermarket.*

---

*Not necessarily a good thing, this third eye. In a Romanian fairy tale, a girl with a third eye—at the back of her neck—ends up getting the hero killed. (He was doing nothing more terrible than getting great gourmet meals out of his magic goat.)

EDITH WALLACE is a lovely woman who worked with Carl Jung in Zürich. She is a painter, a writer, an analyst. Her book, *A Queen's Quest: Pilgrimage for Individuation*, is a beautiful collection of paintings and poetry describing the psychic journey of a woman in search of herself. We sit on a couch in Ark's Alchemy & Psychology section, surrounded by the murmur of three generations of mind trippers. She reminds me of Oneida's Betty Whelan, another luminous presence, the result, no doubt, of years spent in passionate exploration of the mind.

> *For reason is no bridge, is nothing but a barrier,*
> *Really? Reason is so clean, clearcut;*
> *Knowing and understanding such a comfort.*
> *I do not wish to be without reason—*
> *Cool comfort without danger—*
> *Let me have both and be content with the dilemma.*
> Edith Wallace, from *A Queen's Quest*

Edith frowns when I ask her about the feverish New Age business going on all about her. I take her frown to mean there's not much "reason" in the lot of them. But then, she outshines them all with a mysterious light. She is content with the dilemma.

LEANING against a bookcase at Ark, a middle-aged cowboy looks about him as if the people in the store were a book. Robert Petro sees the future. He's found murderers for the police and runaway spouses. He studies my forehead as if it were tomorrow's sports page of the newspaper. How far ahead of the newspaper is he? Can he really tell who'll win the NBA? And if he could why isn't he rich? Can any soothsayer tell for that matter? In a country where the future becomes instantly past and the past is just barely digested future, prophecy is a risky business. He may even be creating the future he claims he is only reading. He's quite a folksy guy, though, and well disposed toward fellow men.

The "gift," as everyone around here calls psychic ability, whether it's soothsaying, forecasting, or the laying on of hands, is something that doesn't seem to discriminate by social class. Petro looks like a cowboy car salesman hustler out of mid-America's endless store of lost-and-found souls. But while the "gift" may not discriminate, the practice of it harkens strictly to the practitioner's class. Finding bodies for the police is mid-American roving-hustler work. Finding the "queen" in woman, as Edith Wallace does, is upper-class European, light medieval—a tapestrylike "search." The plain folk, like Robert Petro, dwell among the mysteries as if they were sitting at the kitchen table. The intellectuals chase after them as if they were astral restaurants.

Beth Pierson

I MEET Beth Pierson at the Ark's jewelry counter.

AC: *Is there something you're looking for?*

BETH: *Oh, I'm just looking at jewelry. I was looking for space-craft earrings. I've had contact with some of the beings that are visiting the planet. A lot of people are having that experience now. And I know it sounds very science fiction, but it's a very common kind of experience that people have.*

AC: *Tell me, what kind of beings?*

BETH: *Some of these particular beings were extremely tall, some of*

Beth Pierson and I at Ark Books in Santa Fe, looking to see if one of the aliens Beth is familiar with will appear.

Lisa Law

them I now realize are a very common variety of the short gray guys with the big eyes.

AC: *What are they looking for over here?*

BETH: *Their race is genetically in trouble and there's a lot of evidence—I mean, there's really no question about it—that they are doing hybrid experiments between the earth humans and their own race, trying to improve their line.*

AC: *You don't seem particularly distressed by what some would construe as an alien invasion. I mean, shouldn't we call the Pentagon?*

BETH: *It can be, obviously, a very frightening experience. I mean, you've got these people showing up in your bedroom in the middle of the night, and they're taking you out of your bed into this strange place and doing these weird medical things to you. Yeah, it can be very frightening. I . . . trust them for some reason.*

Beth is surrounded by aliens. I am one—a Transylvanian Jew from New Orleans in a New Mexican spiritual supermarket, a kid in the multicultural candy shop.

What should I buy? Some more confidence at the wheel would be nice. The Caddy's been acting funny: I tried to stop the day before and it started skidding. That's not a problem Beth can help me with. Her aliens are too serious. I do hope that her operation by the alien doctors was successful. Others were not so lucky: Jesse Helms, David Duke, Patrick Buchanan, William Kilpatrick—they didn't come out so well.

Writer-in-the-Window

AT Zia's Diner in Santa Fe there is a Writer-in-the-Window. Georgelle Hirliman sits there while passersby slip her questions through a slot. She taps her answers in poetry on her little word processor and tapes them to the window. There is usually a crowd out there, letting out hoots and hollers of satisfaction. All around Georgelle people eat nouvelle cuisine and drink expensive water. Bits of conversation drift over the Writer-in-the-Window bent obliviously over her task of shedding light.

This is what I hear from a nearby table, while I stand in line to hand her my questions: "Well, the reason I came back here from California is because I was a Zuni in a past life, and the pull was just too much." After a pause, her table mate rejoinders in an equally matter-of-fact way, "I gave up sex about two years ago because I was a Roman rapist in the past. I'll be a monk next time around." They clink their Perrier glasses thoughtfully. I hand Georgelle my questions. They are:

1. What in tarnation is an American, and what kind am I?
2. What happens to a foreign accent in an American car?
3. If you didn't first have sex in a car, what can you do to make up for it?

Answers:

1. An American is a free being. Unfortunately not enough Americans know this. You, Andre, are a real American, in that you live freely, that is to say, free to be your creative real self.
2. It shines and thinks of itself as glamorous. It then begins to attract American paramours.
3. By now, if you've never ever had sex in a car, especially to break your virginity, you need to have a sofa made of a vintage Ford or Chevy backseat, and practice this great lovemaking tradition in your own living room. Then graduate to your real car backseat.

Good try. Nice work. I think I'll try that.

SANTA FE, I am told over and over, is a gate for extraterrestrials. It is. It's also a rich folks' playground, a Hollywood home away from home, an artist colony, and, lately, the Mecca for thousands of people dying of AIDS who are coming here to find comfort and belief in the afterlife being peddled here. At premium prices.

Foster, My Mother

I AM now at the point in the trip when I am beginning to have serious doubts about the sanity of any Americans, including myself. You don't have to be kidnapped by aliens to be tortured by either doubts or certainties. But I'm determined to follow through with all of Lisa Law's psychic tour. I go to see Foster Perry, psychic healer and rebirther. Maybe the only way I can be healed is to be born again.

In spite of my (still) healthy skepticism, Foster is making the hairs on my arms stand when he begins—from the moment we come through the door—to read me like a book. I feel *leafed* through. He keeps up an incessant patter in a variety of tones, accents, and loudnesses as if voices are *pouring* through him. He's accurate about things I already know, like my problem with my father, but he describes them in uncanny detail as if he's watching a movie being projected on my face. He is trying to cure me from the trauma of driving my father's car into a window when I was a child. He also mentions things that he couldn't possibly know, like my son's Italian girlfriend. Now there is a detail. I wonder if he's also right about things I don't know. Do I really want to know them?

FOSTER: *You replay the past incident of your father in the car and change the ending.*

FOSTER: *We have to ride the car together, my father and I, but this time I'm driving.*

AC: *Are you seeing my guides? Do you see them?*

FOSTER: *Yes.*

AC: *What are they?*

FOSTER: *There are so many, I just told you some of them. The man of the forest is not a guide. It's you.*

AC: *Should I leave the car here then?*

FOSTER: *He tells you, "Now ride the car." "I'm learning to drive the*

Foster Perry,
my Santa Fe mother,
who rebirthed me.

Foster Perry,
my Santa Fe mother,
who rebirthed me.

car now, I do learn to do that. I'm doing it for my sons even though
they want to go over the edge too. And here I will learn how to drive
in America. My soul, my inner life, and my dreams, oh." This is a big
deal.

Foster has written a twenty-five-page-long analysis of my name,
which he performs for me at great speed, gesticulating wildly all the
while. After his energetic performance, I tell him that I invented my
name. He doesn't lose any sleep over that one. "It's your name now.
You made it up, you wear it!" There is just a bit of Brooklyn accent,
and I hear, "You break it, you buy it!" Well then, Foster offers me some
gifts: an ear of corn, a leaf. I give him a gift, as per Ms. Law's
instructions. ("Never see a psychic without a gift.") After this ceremony, we get down to the main business: rebirthing.

Foster makes me lie down on a mat, and then begins to instruct me
to breathe in a circular fashion, and to imagine a variety of colors,
flows, circuits. I follow him pretty easily until I am actually in some
kind of trance. It is at that point that he starts to hurt me. It's a massage
of some kind that penetrates all my muscle tissues deeply.

I'm wincing from pain when he begins to guide me through the womb. It's the first month of my intrauterine life. I'm a baby all right, though for reasons of dignity I'm keeping my mustache. . . . I'm a baby Stalin floating in amniotic fluid . . . now I'm an amoeba-size beam of light swelling to fill up the whole booming ocean cavity . . . get me outta here . . . but it's only the second month! And then the third! It's an excruciatingly slow gestation and I am experiencing anxiety, impatience, and claustrophobia inside my mother. That much for the lost paradise of uterine life! It's hot and crowded in the womb, and I get bigger and bigger . . . I want to grow up quick and get out of my mother's womb as soon as possible . . . my mother's womb isn't half as comforting as Rendelman's caves . . . I want out, I want to grow big enough to get in my Caddy and split this unsteady rocking popcorn joint! And then, finally, it's the seventh or eighth month and I'm born, prematurely, and I find myself curled up rigidly in fetal position in the arms of a sweating, crying Foster, who holds me, saying over and over: *It's all right! Mommy's here! Mommy's here!*

I CAME slowly to, wincing and reeling from pain, feeling as if I'd flown one hundred billion miles in an hour. I stumbled outside into the night to breathe fresh air and look at the stars. I felt like a baby, weak, helpless, strangely undone. Lisa Law came after me and said, "If you need suck, baby, I'll give you suck!" Lisa's maternal offer struck me as very funny, and I laughed until I came back to earth. It was sweet of Lisa to offer, though, with a camera watching and all.

There is a Romanian curse, "Du-te-n mă-ta!," which means, politely, "Go back into your mother!," that is, you're so stupid you ought to get born again. (There is a less polite form, of course.) Well, I had gone into my mother again, and on TV too! But strange as this particular procedure was, it was in fact the American experience *par excellence:* getting born again, over and over. From Romanian to American, from easterner to westerner, from radio to TV, being born again was not only my personal *métier* but the spiritual pastime of every American. I am not that man any longer, officer, reverend, darling, dear universe! It's my American *right* to be reborn, hallelujah!

Chris Griscom

I AM now going to pay homage to the woman who got me off meat. Chris Griscom's Light Institute in Galisteo, New Mexico, is a collection of buildings flooded with light on top of a mountain. The day we arrived, everything was bathed in a brilliant New Mexico light, the texture of which is like gossamer, both physical and unreal. Chris wasn't about yet, but a number of very pretty blond German girls were cheerily running about the immaculate rooms.

Chris Griscom is a past-life reader, a death worker, and an all-around psychic healer. Famous for books like *The Healing of Emotion: Awakening the Fearless Self,* she is a world traveler and a reputed immortal who has had six near-death experiences. She has also given birth in the ocean, an experience she documented in a book of photographs called *Ocean Born.* Giving birth in the ocean has now become something of a fad, which is funny because, as Chris tells it, she herself did it because she had heard that Maori women gave birth in the ocean. A year after she delivered her baby in an inland sea of the Bahamas' Exuma cays, she met a Maori holy man. She told him what she had done in imitation of Maori women. The holy man took a dismayed step backward and stared at her with unadulterated horror, *"We don't do that!"* he shouted. *"Our gods do that! In the stories!"* The gentle self-irony with which Chris tells this story is a good gauge of her person. She is possessed of a truly gracious lightness and a preternatural calm.

She floated in, dressed in white, and asked me to disrobe and lie down on a narrow couch under a skylight. She sat in a chair at the foot of the couch by my head, and started to pull gently on my earlobes, and push at points in my neck and shoulders.

CHRIS: *Now draw the white light into the top of your head and extend it out to your solar plexus. And as you draw it in and extend it out, allow all the images of that lifetime to lift up out of your body.*

SINCE I had been born again, it had gotten easier to let go of my conscious mind. Chris Griscom's hands had to be the most soothing

*Chris Griscom in front of her Light Institute in Galisteo,
New Mexico. Chris guided me through the death of a past
incarnation, and changed me definitively from carnivore to
herbivore.*

instruments I had ever felt. She pushed light through me. She asked
me to describe the hypnagogic apparitions that soon became present
behind my eyelids. I would have liked to describe more poetically the
images I saw (still aware, but not for long, of the camera) but I could
only say from within my light trance words that arose spontaneously
like multicolored bubbles. I was entirely without the will to dissimu-
late. My inner journey mirrored in a funny way my outer one, only
instead of a Cadillac I was driving a sliver of blue light across snow.
. . . I was about to experience a past life, and death.

I SAW a scribe seated in a public plaza in medieval Spain. He was writing letters for people who paid him for it—love letters, news of deals concluded. Under his sheets of parchment there was a stone on which he inscribed simultaneously a cuneiform script that was his *real* work. "How does he feel?" Chris asked me. He was sad, alone, ascetic, preoccupied. "How did he die?" Chris asked gently. He was thin and in his mid-sixties when he lay down on his narrow cot in a modest, spare, monastic room. He crossed his arms peacefully, and died. I died with him, and I was flooded by a great burst of joyous light as he and I—or he as I—let go and floated off into a vastly happy and relaxed blue space. . . .

> CHRIS: *Now go again back to the end of this life. Does it feel powerful, does it feel safe? What is it like?*
>
> AC: *No problem. He dies very easily.*
>
> CHRIS: *Good. It's a beautiful, beautiful death.*

Once more, as I had done after Foster's rebirthing, I had quickly to get outside into the fresh air. I experienced great peace. I walked about on unsteady new legs and felt, how shall I say? great understanding and love. It's hard for me to describe such things because willy-nilly I must fall on a simplified language. But there is no other way to explain this. Even the crew, who had maintained their New York skepticism for as long as they could, began to feel something.

Roger asked Chris: "Does this stuff work on everybody?" (meaning: on tough, cynical New York Jews), and she said: "Yes. It might take awhile if there is resistance, but yes, it works." She pointed out what she said was the light around my face as I staggered out, and they all had to admit they saw it, even Dan. I had no cravings for anything but water for many hours. The euphoria went on for days. I felt that it was OK to die. Make room for new things. Chris works with dying people, and must be a great comfort to them. We are all dying, though, and she certainly was a great comfort to me.

I don't know if it was the combined effect of the New Mexico light, the magic of the landscape, the touching and relaxation, the hypnotic beauty of spiritual chanting and poetry, the attraction of the Elsewhere, but I was beginning to shed my old skin. I resolved never to eat meat again after seeing Chris. I don't really know why. I haven't eaten any since. I will say, if asked, that I don't eat anything that screams when it dies so you can hear it. But, in truth, I don't know why. I got up from Chris's couch a vegetarian.

Alan Olken, Astrologer

IN the space of two days, I was born again, died, came back again—what a country!

My Caddy should have been tired by now. After all we were halfway across the North American continent. Some of the side effects of the curious operations I was undergoing must have been benefiting its cogs and wheels. Its dials shone as if they had been freshly scrubbed, though no one had laid sponge or rag on them for weeks. The only time the Caddy became ill-tempered was when I tried to stop at a small Catholic church. The wheels started spinning, the car fishtailed, and I was unable to stop. Organized religion appeared to be out of the question.

I saw other miracle workers in the next few days, some uncannily accurate, others uncannily inaccurate, or, worse, phony, but they were all entertaining.

Alan Olken, an astrologers' astrologer who counts among his clients politicians and movie stars, looked and sounded as if he could have been a senator, an adviser to the President, or a movie star himself. It was unfathomable to me why he was an astrologer, unless the stars had decreed it, of course. I took full advantage of his trenchant intelligence to find out what the stars had in store for America. The news, I'm afraid, was not very good. He forecast unrest in the cities (before the Los Angeles riot); the reelection of George Bush, who would serve but a short time; and the ascension of Dan Quayle. President Quayle? I hoped Alan was wrong. (He was.)

For me, personally, he forecast sentimental and emotional trouble (what else is new?) and told me that to reach perfection I would have to give up sex. Sure! Meat, OK. But I draw the line at sex. I still don't know why Alan was trying to withdraw me from the gene pool. Orders from the Dark Side, prob'ly.

Christian fundamentalists call all New Age practices, without exception, the Devil's Work. That's about as unfair as the New Age practitioners themselves calling all their practices One Single Art. At least some of them must be the Devil's Work. Others are just Houdini's legacy. And as for the fundamentalists themselves, who's to say if it isn't *they* who are the Devil's Work? The Devil works in mysterious ways. I did not presume to know how Alan knew what he knew. He scared me good about my country, and, oh, about myself. That we all are scary and sublime is no surprise to me but that he knew when and how the fear and the sublimity would manifest . . . that's eerie.

Sheila Channels Theo

SHEILA LOWRY channels an entity called Theo. She has written several books dictated by Theo, including one about the aliens among us, which seem to be unanimously believed in by all New Mexican psychics and healers. Sheila lives in a posh middle-class house in a suburb, and she is a well-groomed, fashionably dressed, and friendly person with a chic dog and a large fireplace. She told me that she had been, for the longest time, exactly what she appeared to be now, that is, a middle-class, well-off idle woman. One day, however, she began to hear voices. Her husband had her committed to a mental hospital. Therapy, including drugs and electroshock, didn't work. The voices kept coming through more clearly and more authoritatively. Sheila left her old life behind and came to Santa Fe, where she met a man (now her husband) who understood the reality of her extrasensorial experience. And the business potential. Now Sheila channels Theo for people who need answers to their questions. Theo is a corporate entity, several spirits which have merged for the purpose of warning and advising humanity.

It is the first instance I know of the corporate world having penetrated the Beyond.

It's my chance to speak to my dead friends if perchance Sheila Lowry's Theo can access them. Spirits it seems all know each other. They must have these huge parties where everybody gets introduced. Sheila's head falls slightly to her chest, and her voice changes to a deep baritone, but is still, recognizably, Sheila's voice. Unfortunately, Theo uses the royal "we" (or perhaps only the corporate "we") and speaks with a ponderous German accent. It is rather impatient with personal questions about my dead friends, one of whom he believes is still alive. I switch the subject to world affairs, an area Theo seems at home with, but he talks like an editorial from *The Washington Post*, only he's even more full of generalities, as well as a pricked and self-righteous irritation at my visible disbelief.

It occurs to me that even if Theo were real (as opposed to a table-turning late nineteenth-century trick of the kind Houdini loved to debunk) he wouldn't be a very good or persuasive thinker and talker. The spirit world, just like ours (only more so) must abound in the untalented, ungifted, pretentious, and ambitious. After all, why would death change all that? According to the Buddhists, assholes stay assholes for myriads of incarnations before their assholeness starts to give a little.

My dead friends Jeff Miller, Ted Berrigan, Darrel Gray, and Glen Knudsen wouldn't sit with Theo for a second—just because they're dead it doesn't mean that they've lost their senses. It amazes me, Theo, the effrontery of presumed intimacy! So, you're familiar with aliens, Atlantis, the Fourth World, the Heavenly Gates, and Saturday-morning cartoons . . . but have some manners. *Please!*

Cherokee

CHEROKEE is a crystal healer. She calls her crystals her babies. In the middle of her living room stands a big copper pyramid surrounded by "babies" of different weights and sizes. Cherokee herself is a healthy red-haired woman in her mid-fifties with a strong southern accent who was once part of Howard Hughes's stable of beautiful women, out of which came a number of stars, a number of models, some chorus girls, and one crystal healer. She is disarmingly frank, folksy, and funny. She readily admits to having no idea how the crystals do their job, but they do, and she tells some very droll stories of old men cured of impotence and gout by the "babies."

Cherokee, crystal healer from Santa Fe. She is guided by
Ariel, a ten-foot angel with long blond hair.

I lay down naked under the copper pyramid while Cherokee chanted
a prayer in a language that sounded like a combination of Hebrew and
Pig Latin. She then conversed briefly with her adviser, Ariel.

CHEROKEE: *Just relax. These crystals have been doing this job for*
a long time now. They really do know what they're doing.
I merely follow orders, place the stones, and get out of the way and
let the energy move.
This is going to go right here. No, just put your legs down. Now,
is the energy coming in, can you feel it yet?

AC: *I can feel something going on.*

CHEROKEE: *Now what do you want to use on his throat? Do you*
want to use that . . . no, I didn't think so. OK, um . . .

AC: *Who are you talking to, Cherokee?*

CHEROKEE: *Archangel Ariel. I've worked with her since about 1975.*

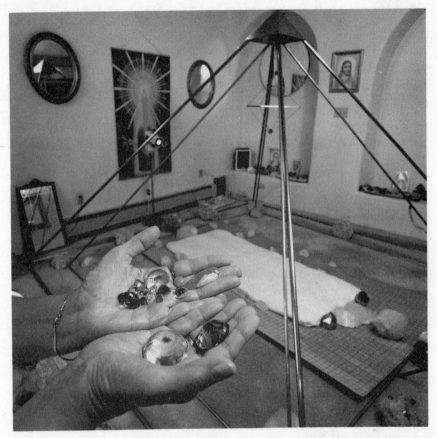

Cherokee's crystals are her "babies." After displaying them to the camera, her hands started to burn.

AC: *Does she have a body like ours?*

CHEROKEE: *Yeah, she has long blond hair. She's a very large being probably eight to ten feet tall. I'm gonna go ahead and start this now. This is the part where it starts getting a little hard for me to stay in here. Whoo. Wow, OK. I don't know whether you'll experience any pain anywhere in the body. If you do breathe green into it and it usually won't last over three or four seconds.*

Cherokee clamped a pair of large, old-fashioned earphones on my head. Celestial Brazilian rhythms intercut with screaming whales came bouncing through. She then turned on her aroma machine and waves of five-and-dime perfumes came wafting into the room. The dentist-office-like heavenly sounds in my ears mixed with the Woolworth-counter scents as Cherokee started sticking crystals into my bodily cavities. She put two little ones in my ears, two littler ones in my nose, and then she inserted a huge one between my legs. On my stomach she laid a humongous one she called "Old Glory." She decorated the rest of me like a Florida souvenir, and made me clutch two crystals in my hands. She then began swinging back and forth a stone as big as Old Glory with both hands, and said: "I'm now going to activate you!"

Old Glory was getting very heavy on my stomach, so I said, "Before you do that, Cherokee, can you move Old Glory? She's getting heavy!" No problem. Cherokee removed Old Glory. Then she activated me. I fell into a profoundly tacky psychic gap, a kind of country-&-western bar in southern Texas.

Crystals must be to the New Age what velvet painting is to art. There's that class thing again. Beautiful. I didn't think I was Elvis in a former life. My chakras were gaping hollows of spiritual disbelief, and I fell asleep.

The Greatest Horror on Earth

DRIVING out of Cherokee's, I watched the sun set over the eerily beautiful New Mexico mountains and thought that an angel must have fallen and burnt hereabouts. There are shards of heaven everywhere—garlands of chili peppers, really.

But this benign angel is not the only one who fell and burned around here. The atomic bomb was developed at Los Alamos and detonated at Alamogordo, New Mexico, not far from where my New Age friends are dreaming about the thousand years of peace of the Aquarian Age.

AT the National Atomic Museum at Kirtland Air Force Base, William Blake's Marriage of Heaven and Hell is consummated. Here on display are Fat Man and Little Boy, the first and only atomic weapons ever used against humans. I look at the horrifying pictures on the walls—

Tour guide at the National Atomic Museum at Kirtland Air Force Base, standing in front of Little Boy, one of the two atomic weapons ever used on human beings.

proud designs and photos documenting the glorious development of the bomb and later bombs. . . .

I'm just another tourist, I think, looking at the greatest horror on earth as if it were just an art show. Just as I dwell on the one, lonely depiction of actual dead humans, a Japanese family—mother, father, two children—pass noisily and touristically through the room, snapping away on their cameras. What kind of art is this to Japanese tourists? I wonder. Postmodern ultrarealism, at the very least.

Easing my transition from the pink-lit vistas of the New Age to the facts and figures of the old one is the Atomic Museum tour guide. She is as enthusiastic about her little evil chamber as a curator at the Louvre. She recites cheerily the weight, width, and length of every bomb in the museum, and their destructive potential, which she calls "fatalities." She must mean human beings.

When I ask her why there aren't more pictures of these weapons' effects on "fatalities," she claims there isn't enough space, and that they wouldn't be appropriate for the "peanut butter-and-jelly age group."

I feel a distinct wave of maleficent particles emanating from every corner of this DOE propaganda chamber, so I ask her if any UFOS have been visiting here.

It's a hopeful question, but she laughs it away. "No, no," she says. Bomb keepers see no aliens. But as for me, I can only hope that some of Beth Pierson's well-meaning aliens are stealthily incapacitating these things.

"I have just learned in Santa Fe that you can have an out-of-body experience without using atomic bombs," I tell her. She pities me.

Biosphere 2

THE Western desert is focusing our millennial aspirations like a telescope lens. The space age that began here with the atomic bomb has put all of us on a cosmic path. The millennial menu is staggering. We are walking a tightrope between destroying ourselves, recovering the old ways, and migrating to the stars. Inner and outer space are fusing in Oracle, Arizona, home of Biosphere 2.

Convinced that life on earth—Biosphere 1—is doomed, eight voluntary hostages have sealed themselves inside a $150 million futuristic bubble for two years.

Trapped inside this more-or-less eco-perfect bubble the biospherians present themselves as pioneers of future life in space, though for the moment they are still on earth and fast on their way to becoming Arizona's second-largest attraction after the Grand Canyon, a Disneyland for the millennially distressed. A tour group goes by, and several people look inside, hoping for a glimpse of a biospherian. One of them points excitedly: "There goes one! I saw it!" Modern lemurs.

Biosphere 2 was financed by a reclusive billionaire named Ed Bass,

Biosphere 2 in Oracle, Arizona. Preparing to leave the planet.

and is the brainchild of John Allen, the visionary leader of a religious sci-fi cult that began as a hippie psychodrama commune.

Mark Nelson is Director of Space Applications and Communications System Manager. Not yet able to beam aboard, I go for the next best thing: a walkie-talkie. We communicate through the glass.

AC: *Would you tell me why in the world you would get in there and stay in there for years?*

MARK: *If we're really going to live in space, not just go out there with our picnic lunches to make footprints on the moon or Mars, we're going to need to take robust living systems. We're going to need to miniaturize biospheres.*

Mark Nelson, biospherian, looking out of his glass prison. Or spacecraft.

AC: *What sort of utopia is this? What is the faith that it's based on?*

MARK: *Personally, I grew up in the sixties. And the sixties I think, you know, really did make a big consciousness change around the planet. And certainly growing up in that time, I was determined that I would be—in the phrase of the time—part of the solution, not of the problem. My reading of history is that we have a limited number of scripts, and most of them have fairly sad endings. In a way we need*

new scripts, and if we are going to take our life and our fellow species
with us in space we are going to need to take biospheres with us.

Once more, visions of stirpiculture dance before my eyes as I behold
the lily-white version of the future in Oracle, Arizona. Yet . . . there
is undeniable pathos in being trapped in a bubble for years like Captain
Nemo, a futuristic bubble being who may die instantly on impact with
the future upon emergence, as new generations of germs and viruses
unknown to him are waiting to pounce!

Even though I'm not sure I'm on earth anymore, Mark Nelson and
I also talk about William Burroughs, whom Nelson had been reading
and admiring. The very same Burroughs who is also on the minds of
Taos Pueblo Indians. The author of *Naked Lunch* spans worlds.

"The earth is an Indian thing."

Walking through the redwoods one moonless night in northern
California, I felt both the vastness and the tenderness of this orb. I
wrote:

> *The trees may be scary,*
> *but hidden among them*
> *is your house.*

One biosphere is enough for me. Even if everybody takes off for
outer space, I think I'll stay here.

Further

WILLIAM CARLOS WILLIAMS, born of a Spanish mother and an
American father, wrote:

> *The beauties of travel*
> *are due*
> *to the strange hours*
> *we keep*
> *to see them.*

The West was made for riding. Our heroes spring to life here like saguaro cactus, from the outlaw on his nag to the lowrider on his cholo. Here the Nouveau Americans can practice the Bill of Rights and the Aesthetic of the Baroque—if they like.

In America, you can invent a difference in the A.M. . . . by afternoon it's a tradition . . . by evening it's a market with its own advertising.

The Smithsonian has already enshrined a lowrider in its halls, and as for the New Age, you better hurry, prices are going up as we speak!*

The desert always spoke many languages: Indian tongues, Spanish, English—but it whispered some of them. Now it's beginning to speak them loudly, with a swagger that mixes words from all of them: American Desert Spanish, Spanish-Indian, Anglo-Chicano, Urban Hip Indo-Spanglish, New Age Speak.

Muralistos

I DRIVE on to Arizona. The Southwest is salsa-flavored. I feel like I've driven across the taste buds of America, from the sexless vegetables of the Bruderhof to the chilies of Arizona.

The boiling pot keeps cooking, the food and *colores* are steaming. I converse briefly with a couple of muralists, David Tineo and Antonio Pazos, high on their ladders, painting a fantastic mural on the wall of the Tucson Art Museum. The *muralistos* are highriders. They express on walls what the lowriders express on the road. They are the *los angeles* of the picture story of La Raza. Here come Aztecs, Mayans, Indios, Latin Americans, and Chicanos down the tortured celestial highway, revving their engines of color.

DAVID: *It says a lot, because being at the museum says that not only is the museum for a certain group of people, but for all people. It is also for the Chicano youth to come over here, it's also for the barrio people to come to the museum because this is their museum too.*

AC: *There is anger here too. What is the anger about?*

*It's amazing what a gold mine the Beyond has always been! The West is itself America's Beyond.

DAVID: *I have various teaching degrees, I'm a part-time professor at the college, yet two years ago I was doing a mural and was almost arrested because someone thought I was vandalizing the place. Because of my tattoos, because of the color of my skin. And what we're saying, hey, we have an art form, we have a rich history. Chicano means being proud—who we are, where we come from, and what we've contributed to this country.*

My bright red Caddy looks comfortable here in Arizona. Its color blends easily with the chili-pepper earth and Indian pigments.

Sun City: the Eternal Now

WHAT is this? Easy riders? Hell's Angels? The Dean-Brando gang? The Wehrmacht? No, the riders look clean, the bikes are Japanese, they have their helmets on. They are the Power Riders, who escorted me to Sun City, a paradise for seventy thousand people over fifty-five. What makes it paradise is precisely the absence of unsettling young people whose arrogantly taut flesh reminds everyone of mortality.

Nobody in America wants to die anymore—except perhaps at the hands of Chris Griscom.

RIDER 1: *Well, a lot of us have ridden for many years. I've ridden a bike for forty, forty-five years.*

RIDER 2: *I've ridden a bike for fifty-eight years.*

AC: *Does this keep you young?*

RIDER 1: *Oh, I haven't gotten old yet.*

We converse about life and they all declare their allegiance to the life in the Eternal Now. If they have regrets, if they have bad dreams, if they saw the ruin of war or the collapse of civilization, that's all water under the bridge now. What matters is the weather and that someone keep the golf course eternally green. My mother lives in one of these

*The Power Riders of Sun City, Arizona. These senior citizen
bikers were recently reborn to be wild.*

places in Florida, though not quite as affluent as this one. When I visit
her I cringe by the gates at all the medical offices with their doctor
signs surrounding the old like fat buzzards. My mother hates it, she
says it's for old people, and she doesn't feel old.

I took a walk from her apartment one time and got lost. I passed
through dozens of identical setups, buildings with a patch of green and
a swimming pool, a few tables where old folks in Florida polka dots and
stripes sat playing cards, streets named after tropical islands, buildings
named after tropical drinks, apartment numbers using both letters and
numbers. I felt that I had wandered into a mirrored world, a hell for
people we don't want to see anymore. It took days, it seemed, to find
my mother on Kileua Street, Mai Tai Bldg, 12K7K. She was there,
luckily, watching golf on TV.

Sun City, where everyone else's mother lives, is yet another Heavenly Jerusalem promising that wrinkles will be ironed out, warts

exiled, ailments banished, and complaints cauterized by the magic of sun and enforced leisure. The Angel of American Death limps outside the gates of Sun City, too weak to knock. And even if it did, it wouldn't be heard anyway.

One Foot in the Grave, Sun City's punk rock band, led by an ex-mortician, Jo-Dina Errichetti, is jamming. Everyone is wearing T-shirts from Jo-Dina's family's funeral home.

AC: *So, what's it like living here with all these old people. You seem to have so much more energy than anybody I've ever seen.*

JO-DINA: *We are the youngsters.... (To the band) You guys are the youngsters of Sun City, right?*

Jo-Dina Errichetti, lead vocalist for "One Foot in the Grave," Sun City's punk band.

GENE (drummer): *To get into Sun City you have to be fifty-five.*

JO-DINA: *But isn't age, you know, all in the mind?*

GENE: *Age means a lot. Lumbago, heart attacks, no lungs, cataracts.*

AC: *Is this the American dream incarnate? Are you living it?*

JO-DINA: *I guess that is America. You can do anything you want to do at any age and . . . I'm not even a singer and I'm the lead.*

GUITARIST: *Vocalist.*

JO-DINA: (laughs) *They won't let me say I sing.*

They sing "Menopause," a pathos-filled, jarring ditty about the evils of old age. Jo-Dina falls to the floor with a dramatic flourish, her leather miniskirt and high heels punkishly askew.

Whew!

The war against death takes no prisoners. Banished, sanitized, terror-stripped, domesticated, and painless, American death barely limps behind these valiant positive thinkers. Though I work in the hospices of the business of death, I fear no cosmic despair, for America is with me! The enemies are many—the worst is youth. The arrogant young. Our children are vultures perched on the hills ready to pick our bones and pockets clean. . . . We'll see about that!

Caddy Pushes On

THE true American religion is speed. When you go fast you don't notice much. In the Church of Speed, Inattention is God. If you go fast enough, you'll take the approximate over the accurate . . . the copy over the original . . . the copy of the copy over the copy . . . the ideal cowboy over the bone-tired cowpoke . . . the mythic gunslinger over the petty criminal . . . the illusion over reality . . . the fast buck over the sweaty nickel.

How fast is a fast buck? That's the question. There is nowhere to go and everything to believe. You weren't born when the West was wild? No problem. Dreaming of wild women? Here is Calamity Jane, roadside attraction, Rawhide Western Theme Park. The first time around, history is a drag. The next time around, it's entertainment. Getting shot was once a drag? No problem. We fixed that, kids. Cowboy Fights. Another roadside attraction. Hawkers, con men, drunks, brawlers, card sharps, carnival freaks, thieves, roadside preachers, smooth talkers, floozies, quick-change artists, gunslingers, and dealers in heavenly real estate: our history's full of them. Here they are, stripped of their noxious influence, toys of the imagination, models for children.

WHEN night falls on the back roads of America, the lights of kitsch, simulacra, and a desperate good time come on. This is an inhabited country, cry the lonely motels . . . there is good company to be found at the next stop.

But this is cold light. There is no one out here really, there are no people behind the signs, and the ones there are are empty and lonely like the signs. Cold neon invents a world that isn't there.

There is so much room in the vasty empty neon North American continent. Bring on the Romanians . . . the Haitians . . . the Pakistanis. There is room for Palestine and Kurdistan here. Fill the night with ethnic restaurants.

So I thought, driving past fake Indian trading posts, grotesque museums, kitsch western history, gas food lodging, and immense darkness . . . all the way to Las Vegas.

Vegas: The Kingdom of If

THE people of Sun City are long-suffering Americans who found, a bit late, the root of all evil: boring work. They won't do it anymore, and who can blame them?

But they could have thought of it sooner. Well, some people have thought of not doing any work at all—and are dreaming that the Goddess of Luck is smiling kindly on them her smile of neon and glitz. Las Vegas writes on the sky with neon and she says: Come here, ye wretched of nine-to-five jobs, and see if you weren't intended for something better! See if perchance fate has cheated you out of your due; come see if you can overcome the dirty trick that has kept you down; come be what you never were but that you could be if . . . if only if . . .

Vegas is the Kingdom of If. Come forth, all ye schmoes and suckers, to the neon shores of the American Dream. This is where you can get your reward right away, in this life, without waiting for the next. Of course, the people with real money, the mostly Mormon bankers of Vegas, neither gamble nor drink nor fornicate. They watch over you with benign contempt in their eyes.

I should know.

FIRST time I hit Vegas was in the mid-seventies with two poets, Gene R. and Suzy S. We were there to hold poetry sessions in local high schools in and around Vegas. In Vegas was OK, but *around* Vegas covered a few thousand square kilometers, which necessitated the use of a car. I didn't drive. Suzy didn't have a license. Gene had one but

*Elvis in his Vegas dressing room preparing to release
America's pent-up nostalgic sentimentality.*

it had been revoked by the police for drunken driving. The Nevada
Arts Council put us up in a big casino hotel. The next thing I knew it
was about 4 A.M. and we were buying drinks for drunk salesmen from
the Midwest and charging them to the Arts Council. After that, I
remember losing the $100 I had on me to two hands of blackjack. In
the morning, which came a few minutes later, a man arrived with an
official State of Nevada car for us to drive into the blazing sun into the
desert somewhere. Green, weary, nauseated, and weak, the three unli-

censed drivers took to the road to nowhere. We passed Hoover Dam, a monstrous structure set for no good reason in the middle of the desert, and then backed up to it for bodily functions. We peed and some of us puked into the black marble bathrooms that were like devil's mirrors.

Vegas impersonator, humble servant of Beauty.

After many hours of being roasted on solar spits of pain we pulled into a high school and stood before hundreds of bewildered young faces crowded into a courtyard surrounded by loudspeakers. We climbed on a sort of cloth-covered scaffold with microphones. I remembered vaguely the purpose of our journey. "What is poetry?" I asked. Nobody knew. Not the kids. Not Gene, who looked dead. Not Suzy, who was the oddest shade of transparent viridian. "Poetry is suffering," I said. They could relate to that. Then I got defiant. "But it's also the right to say Fuck you! to Suffering. It's the right to look Suffering in the eye and to say, Fuck you, Suffering! Piss, shit, puke on you, Suffering!" I worked myself up to some truly lyrical heights before I noticed the worried teachers herding their charges out of there. Before long, we

Vegas beauty, continued.

stood in some kind of purgatory-colored office before the principal, a trembling English teacher, and Senator Alan Bible (RIP), Democrat of Nevada. The senator said, "Don't let the sun set on you in Nevada, boys!"

Suzy started to cry because he'd called her "boy." We drove back to Vegas a little older but suffering a little less—the prospect of medicinal drinks ahead making us feel quite cheery, actually—and we arrived just as the neon lit up, a magnificent sight at sunset. In the parking lot,

we met two young hustlers named Happy Jack and Good Time
Charlie. They had gotten themselves into a bit of a jam, just like us.
It seems that they had just cracked a safe in one of the big casinos with
liquid nitrogen when they were caught by the police. Mercifully, the
cops only took the money they had just taken out of the safe, and had
told them, quoting someone: "Don't let the sun set on you in Nevada,
boys." They had no problem with that, but they would rather go early
next morning than right away, so could we put them up in our rooms?
That was fine with me. Happy Jack and Good Time Charlie were
actually pretty amusing, and we stayed up most of the night ordering
room-service drinks and food, because we were all broke. In the morning, the two guys got up before everyone else. I watched them from
the window hotwire a silver Porsche and take off. We left town shortly
after, by plane.

That was the first time. The next few times were less colorful, but
each one had its story, and each story ended with my leaving everything I came with at the blackjack tables. And sometimes money I
didn't come with. I finally made my peace with Vegas years later when
I went to read poetry there as a guest of the local public radio station.
I played monk that time, was moderate in all things, saw "Nudes on
Ice & Steak = $9.99," and lost but a modest C-note.

And there was even a good moment. In 1986, I took my mother
there. She put all the childish faith of her unhappy life into gambling
as if two or three strokes of luck might undo decades of bad breaks. She
lost all her money, and so did I, but we gained each other's company
for three days. It was worth it.

This time, I came to make a movie. And to take on some real pros.
I handed the Caddy to the valet at Caesar's and strode in in grand style.
All I lacked was a cigar but I can't smoke them. I brushed past the
exhausted beauties in last night's velvet gowns and passed without a
glance at the bored hoods the casino keeps on megavitamins by the
fake palm trees.

I threw my chips down. Ten grand.

Three of the guys I sat down to play poker with were world champions. Tank Top Tony tried drugs, alcohol, religion, meditation, and
crime, before settling on gambling. His father was with him, a rum-
pled Brooklyn fellow who also plays poker for a living. Tony likes to
keep dad around, and tells everybody that he owes everything he is to
dad. Dad beamed like the gold wrapper around a fine cigar.

Wayne Newton attempting to triumph over the IRS.

Jay was an anthropology professor who got bored teaching students about human behavior and decided to make a career out of manipulating it at the poker table.

David had never done anything but gamble and was doing time at the tables until he earned enough to find peace.

Well, it is just a job. Maybe not so glamorous as movie star but a heck of a lot closer to it than plumber in Poughkeepsie. Getting to the top in poker is just like getting to the top in IBM; you work hard, set yourself against the odds, and don't give a sucker an even break.

"World-class poker player" seems like a pretty classy title, but these guys have plenty of small-time tics. Jay keeps his money in his socks. Tank Top stashes his cash occasionally in his shoes. We start to play. I have $200 in chips in front of me. I expect to lose just about immediately. These guys doubtless have a special relationship with Lady Luck. Of course, they don't know that before leaving New Orleans I put a chicken foot on Marie Laveau's grave. I have a rabbit foot in the car, a special stone in my pocket. And I'm born again on top of it.

So I draw a hand I think is two pairs. There is a round of raising, and another. It's a pretty good stash there in the middle of the table. When I show my cards, I say: "Two pair." Everyone laughs. What I have is a diamond flush. I didn't know. I win. Maybe there is something in this for me. There is: Roger and Jean are pissed off because at this point in the movie we need a joke and the joke was supposed to be that I lose all my money. Haha. We play another round, and I draw a pair of tens. David raises like crazy but, ugh, everyone stays in. I get three aces when I discard. Everybody checks, I raise a little. They stay in. Phew! Tank Top suddenly raises a lot. Jay drops out. Dad drops out. I see him and raise him. Three raises later everybody's looking at us. The camera's rolling. I spread out my cards. I did it, once again. Jean is disgusted. He stops shooting, and then, of course, I lose the next three games. Everything goes. Well, at least the movie's on my side. Kodak be with you.

DEALER: *We have queens and tens. Two pair.*

AC: *Queens and tens . . . Kings and fours.*

JAY: *You know you can't beat an all-in player.*

AC: *Clearly there is a difference between a schmo like me and a professional player, even if I get lucky once or twice.*

TONY: *I think you're doing real well. I wouldn't mind winning a few pots myself today.*

AC: *Yeah, why did I win?*

JAY: *Tourists win because they're lucky. Professionals win because they're good.*

AC: *Is this a dream come true for you to live this life?*

TONY: *I think that if I had to have a job doing the same thing day in and day out, it would have destroyed me, personally.*

JAY: *I've heard professional players and others talking about how they played for a lifetime, never had a real job. But they're dreaming. They'll come in and they'll put in 180 hours a week playing poker and they'll say, "I never had a job." That sounds to me like a job.*

Vegas night god calling for the sacrifice of a tourist.

DAVID: *My attack is more of a mercenary, whereas I think Tony is still at the stage of some kind of enjoyment. You can tell, he even smiles when he wins. I mean, the man is aglow. Whereas the glow is gone in me. I'm just a hard-nosed professional.*

TONY: *I think most of my knowledge that I obtained throughout life came from playing poker, you know, because I don't do a lot of reading.*

DEALER: *Fours you are high . . . He's got a diamond flush.*

TONY: *Have you ever thought of doing this professionally?*

Luv

THESE guys never see daylight, and try to be as tough as the night can make them. A few doors down, people made sentimental by TV are marrying each other. Here, at the Little White Chapel, is the assembly line of sentiment, Vegas style. Charlette, the Henry Ford of the heart, is the owner and claims she's the minister, too. Both of her get little white envelopes stuffed with the "donations" that the shy lovers fish out of their threadbare pockets and the pockets of their relatives. They get a free photograph, but not a "professional" one. That's extra. Also extra: wedding cake, video or audio tape recording, gown and tux rental, live organ music, bridal bouquet, corsages, boutonnieres, rings, garters, champagne glasses, marriage certificate and holder, and many more wedding mementoes . . . "to make your wedding dreams come true."

Music: "Hawaiian Wedding Song."

ORGAN PLAYER: *I do get choked up. Sometimes I sit here and bawl right along with the people. And it's very touching because most of the couples are so in love, and it's really neat to see 'em.*

CASHIER: *Your total is seventy dollars and forty cents.*

AC: *How long does it take to get married here?*

CHARLETTE: *Five to six minutes. Yeah, about five to six minutes.*

AC: *How is that different from McDonald's?*

CHARLETTE (smiles): *Well, my dear, it's different from McDonald's because we serve hearts full of love, we don't serve hamburgers and french fries.*

*Liberace fan club on the anniversary of his death. Vita brevis,
ars extra-longa.*

AC: *Less fat.*

CHARLETTE: *More hugs . . . more love.*

CASHIER: *Did you have an envelope for the minister's donation?*

CUSTOMER: *Uh, we haven't done that yet.*

CASHIER: *Did you care to give her one?*

CUSTOMER: *Yeah . . .* (forks over bills)

The Little White Chapel and her many sister chapels looking just
like frosty pink Taco Bells or Wienerschnitzels are on a pretty cheesy
street. Across the street are scores of cheap apartment buildings. I see
little kids peering through the curtains at all the weddings. The TV is
on in all the apartments. They too will be married one day.

BARBARA, Charlette's receptionist, whispers to me that she's a Polish writer working here for her book on America. She's undercover, like everyone else, it seems to me. In America we are all aliens with very obvious accents working undercover for the American Dream, in whatever shape—whether the great Polish American novel or the Romanian American search for utopias.

Tom and Kimberly in a hurry to do the right thing at the
Vegas White Chapel drive-by wedding window.

BARBARA (to customer): *We call this Regular Packages for $189, Deluxe $239, also Michael Jordan Special for $389 and the best one, ah, Joan Collins Special $499, which includes totally everything, you can't have more.* (She beams.)

But the ultimate in expedient *amour* is the drive-by wedding— twenty-five bucks a pop. Nondrivers will never experience the quickie bliss of the Vegas-style American wedding. My driver's license gives me undreamt-of bonuses. These Harley-Davidson newlyweds have brought no witnesses.

CHARLETTE: *Welcome to the Little White Chapel Drive-Up Wedding Window. We are gathered here tonight to join you together in marriage. Tom, will you take Kimberly to be your wedded wife?*

TOM: *Yes, I do.*

CHARLETTE: *And, Kimberly, will you take Tom for your husband?*

KIMBERLY: *Yes, I will.*

CHARLETTE: *Well, Tom and Kimberly, what God has joined together let no man take apart. And by the power invested in me by the state of Nevada, you are legally married, husband and wife. Tom, you may now kiss your beautiful bride.*

They kiss for about four seconds.

CHARLETTE: *Let her come up for air!*
  Bye now, stay happy and love each other forever. Bye-bye!

Hollo-Deck

AMERICA is the ultimate hollo-deck. The secret of capitalist happiness is that everyone lives exactly like everyone else. The only difference is that whereas the rich consume expensive items, the poor consume the imitation of those items. The difference between an Armani-suit-clad man wearing a real Rolex and his poorer mirror image in an Armani clone with a fake Rolex is visible only to tailors, watchmakers, and thieves. What's more, the expensive items that guarantee the rich man's authenticity are often inferior in quality to the poor man's. A rich man may be eating an individually wrapped tomato that's an imitation of a real tomato while the poor man may be eating an infinitely tastier home-grown tomato. There is no system of values in place to validate which is the original and which is the copy.

America is a democracy, which means that it's rude to value the original over the copy. But the opposite is not true; Americans value the copy over the original. Elvis is dead (when he died very few people cared any longer whether he was alive or dead) but the Elvis industry lives on. Marilyn Monroe is gone but her look lives forever. Real people are an encumbrance, actually, to the joyful use of the image. The hollo-deck is nice, TV obliterates those pesky differences of personality.

IN America, we don't need surrealist art. America is de facto surrealist. Marcel Duchamp's "Mechanical Bride" is always on call in Vegas.

THE Phoenicians wrote on stone tablets with cuneiform characters. The Egyptians wrote glyphs on papyrus. Vegas writes on the sky with neon. The saints used to wander through the desert because there were no temptations. Well, Bugsy Siegel and Howard Hughes fixed that. Of course, they would have been better saints if they hadn't lost their rags at the poker table.

DRIVE through the desert. Avoid the speed traps. The insane prospectors with beards to the ground and crazed eyes. Charlie Manson's tenth tribe still driving dune buggies through ghost towns built by Hollywood. Rattlesnakes on every cactus waiting for sunset. Emaciated wild horses. Carcasses of everything animal, mechanical, and from space— human skeletons, coyote skulls, car bodies, wrecked UFOs. Nuclear tests underground.

America everywhere you look.

San Francisco

I GOT out of the Nevada crapshoot and headed directly for my past. San Francisco, the golden city of my youth, was the westernmost point of my generational migration. From here on out there is nothing but ocean. You can't run any farther. You must turn around to face yourself. Some people could not take what they saw. They jumped into the ocean or ran back to the landlocked certainties of the Midwest. Others stayed, and made do.

I lived in California from 1970 until 1978—four of those years in San Francisco, where my son Lucian was born, and four in Monte Rio, a little town ninety miles north of San Francisco in the redwood forest on the Russian River, twenty minutes from the Pacific Ocean.

It was a wild time by anyone's standards, and ours weren't exactly those of middle-class America. Communards, poets, mystics, drug casualties, rednecks, and criminals—sometimes all in one person—populated the northern California coast. Monte Rio was a quiet town with the exception of the times when the river flooded, the wooden houses burnt down, and the Hell's Angels came on vacation.

When the Angels came the townspeople barricaded themselves inside their houses and sat with shotguns across their laps until the party was over. When they heard the roar of motorcycles in the distance they emerged to survey the damage. A few buildings burnt to the ground, a couple of bodies on the street—not too bad. The sheriff was headquartered thirty miles away and he preferred not to interfere with vacationing Angels.

My wife, Alice, and my friends Jeffrey Miller, Pat Nolan, Hunce Voelcker, Mary Heyssen, Glen Knudsen, and many others had various

The Pink Elephant in Monte Rio. Rough bar of my youth,
Hell's Angels hangout. Unmatched for playing pool on a
rainy afternoon . . .

hangouts in town, but only Jeffrey, Pat, and I were men enough to
hang out at the Pink Elephant. The Pink, as we called it, had real
swinging western doors, and it was not unusual to see someone fly out
of them face first on a Saturday night. One time Pat and I were having
a quiet pool game in the afternoon at the Pink. There was no one in
the place, unless you count the two burly lumberjacks quietly arm-
wrestling at the bar. Pat and I were playing our usual Monte Rio
weekday-afternoon sleepy and awful game, when the place got suddenly dark and a line of quarters appeared on the side of the pool table.
When I looked up I saw that the whole place had filled with the Hell's
Angels and their mamas. How they got in so stealthily I'll never figure.

Neither Pat nor I heard their usual roar. Needless to say, we both tried our best to lose as quickly as possible since neither one of us cared to play the Angels after they had their first beer. But try as we might, we couldn't sink a single ball. Baffled, several Angels crowded in to give us free lessons. Pat and I looked at each other: it was now or never. We put down our cues, bowed like gentlemen, and walked out of the bar to general titters. I remember thinking just how old these Angels looked. It must be hard, I thought, to keep the flags of rebellion flying when you're a grandfather! Little did I know. Here I am, still flapping the old pennant.

HUNCE VOELCKER, one of my best friends, was a poet and a scholar of the poet Hart Crane, the author of *The Bridge.* In honor of Crane, Hunce built a house that was rife with images and motifs from Crane's poetry. He built a moat with bridges over it, and used ships' cables for banisters inside the house. His little Hartcranian castle was built initially with hitchhiker labor. Hunce gave rides to the numerous hitchhikers who lined the country roads in those days, and asked them if they had any carpentry or masonry skills. In exchange for a place to stay and food, they would work on his house. The trouble was that most of them had no idea what they were doing and made mistakes. Hunce kept a careful log of their mistakes so that the next wave of hitchhiker-builders could follow the original mistakes. In the end, the house cost him three times as much as it would have if he'd hired professionals.

Hunce was a poet and a gentleman, though, and he loved orphans, animals, children, and hitchhikers. He had a huge pet cow named Ocean Peace, who sat in a beautiful barn eating apples and watching TV. Our friend Jeffrey Miller, also a poet, tortured the vegetarian Voelcker by renaming his cow "Big Mac." Both Hunce and Jeffrey are dead. Hunce died in 1990 of emphysema from smoking too many of his hand-rolled cigarettes.

Jeffrey, along with my friend Glen Knudsen, died in a car accident in 1977.

PEOPLE washed up on the shores of California from everywhere. The North American continent was restless. People came in waves. We were driftwood. I often walked on the beaches where the Russian River flowed into the Pacific. Sometimes we built houses from driftwood. All was in flux, temporary, brilliant, alive.

Orpheus watching over my friend Hunce Voelcker's schloss in Monte Rio, California. Hunce was a poet, a scholar of Hart Crane (see the "Brooklyn Bridge" motif of his abode). Hunce succeeded in persuading the Oxford English Dictionary committee to change the definition of the word "uranian." He died of emphysema from smoking too many hand-rolled cigarettes.

IN San Francisco, I pulled directly in to North Beach in front of the City Lights Bookstore. North Beach, like the Lower East Side of New York and the Left Bank of Paris, is one of the capitals of bohemia, the mecca of literal and metaphorical exiles from the status quos of society. City Lights was my college in the early seventies, the shelves were my classes. My fellow students stood before these books, unknown to each other, but linked by a mysterious feeling known only to the intensely shy.

One day I found myself there, graduated. Actually, it was a little more wicked than that. My first book of poetry, *License to Carry a Gun*, had just come out, so I used to stand near it in the bookstore to see who looked at it. (Nobody discernibly bought anything.) If the browser happened to be a dreamy-eyed girl in love with poetry, I would leap like an evil dwarf (no, I'd sidle, actually, or perhaps lope) and tell her that I was the poet. I made her a gift of the book on the spot. I never had any money, so I had to steal it and wait for her outside. We would then go to Café Trieste for espresso and there I would inscribe it for her with words so passionate and poetic she often found it impossible not to make love to me on the spot. Alas. The past is so malleable.

I hoped never to get caught by Mr. Ferlinghetti, the owner of City Lights, because I admired his poetry and I would have died from the disgrace. I did get a contemptuous answer once from the manager, Shig, who said in answer to my question about when exactly was he going to reorder my book: "Never. That book gets stolen too fast!" I protested most vehemently. Was it my fault that people loved it enough to steal it? I failed to mention my small contribution.

Lawrence Ferlinghetti published Allen Ginsberg, Jack Kerouac, and Frank O'Hara under the imprint of City Lights Books. Out of his hands came the small spring of rebel writing that became the mighty river of the sixties. I had but two ambitions when I left Romania: to be published in English by City Lights, and in French by Gallimard. The first one is done. City Lights published my memoir, *In America's Shoes*, and an anthology from my literary journal *Exquisite Corpse*, called *The Stiffest of the Corpse: an Exquisite Corpse Reader*.

Ferlinghetti is a terribly private person. He doesn't like to be bothered, but we managed to invade him anyway. What did he think of America now, I asked him, as opposed to Kerouac's America. Kerouac's trip, like mine, had San Francisco as its terminus.

AC: *Lawrence, I'm driving through America like Jack Kerouac . . . and I thought that I would come and pay my respects to you . . . and see if you'll publish my book about it.*

FERLINGHETTI: *A new* Naked Lunch.

AC: *Nothing naked about it so far, alas! But I'm here at last, the end of America, the Westest of the West. . . .*

FERLINGHETTI: *San Francisco is gradually separating itself from the rest of the United States. It's the old Indian myth of San Francisco as an island, it's going to come true in the twenty-first century. You know, South San Francisco is only a foot above sea level, and the icebergs melting and the temperature of the earth rising and the seas rising, it's gonna come through South San Francisco, and this will be an island, as it was in prehistoric times. And so then San Francisco will declare itself an independent city-state, and they won't allow any new automobiles to come on the island, and generally the old automobiles will rot away, and the citizens will plant great gardens on the free-ways, and that'll be it, I mean, it's part of the deconstruction of our world, I mean, it has begun, the deconstruction of all the empires, like beginning with the Ottoman empire. Deconstruction isn't just fashion-able in linguistics departments and art, it's in geopolitics. So you have the deconstruction of all the empires. The Ottoman empire, the British empire, the French empire. And recently the Soviet empire. And now, next, it will be the deconstruction of the American empire. So you'll have gradually states and territories of the United States detaching themselves from the main body, Puerto Rico becoming independent, Alaska becoming independent, California dividing into two states, Northern and Southern California, there's a movement again to do that. In Sacramento now there's a bill in the legislature to divide north and south California again. And then, San Francisco becoming an independent city-state is part of the same thing. The geological drift is making everything west of the San Andreas fault separate from the mainland anyway, so everything is going in that direction, and the anarchist ideal will take over in the end. It's a pure anarchist idea, deconstruction.*

AC: *Well, I always thought that San Francisco had detached itself from the mainland United States in the 1960s, and that the big*

Lawrence Ferlinghetti, poet, publisher, pacifist, anarchist. City Lights Bookstore, the center of planetary hip bohemia, is behind him.

earthquake already happened and that we are all living a post-mortem existence here in paradise. . . . Is that why Kerouac came here?

FERLINGHETTI: *The road hardly exists anymore, it's all up in the air. The youth of the country don't see the land anymore, they just fly from place to place, and it's part of the disappearance of the outside that you wrote about. I mean, there is nothing out there anymore. All in their TV heads. I don't know what Kerouac would have done today, but, I mean, Kerouac was a late-comer on the road. . . . Jack London was on the road, and what about Henry Miller's* The Air-Conditioned Nightmare? *I mean, Henry Miller drove across the country during the Second World War, when he had to leave France, and he went from New York to the West Coast in an old car and wrote* The Air-Conditioned Nightmare. *That was the beginning of the vision which Kerouac really elaborated on, and it was much more potent in Henry Miller as far as I'm concerned. Miller was more focused on the reality of America whereas Kerouac was off in his Catholic consciousness more. When you read* On the Road *closely, you see he really wasn't observing the reality in front of him. He was doing this being on the road at the very end of the forties, or the early fifties, and the America Kerouac saw was the 1930s, a pre–World War II America. That's why there's such nostalgia, or why Kerouac is very popular today. . . .*

It seems to me there's this nostalgia for a pre–World War II America that doesn't even exist anymore, except in forlorn, lost Greyhound bus stations and small towns out back. You get a glimpse of the 1930s America, which was really the America of Thomas Wolfe, and the America that Thomas Wolfe's hero, Eugene Gant, saw in Look Homeward, Angel *when he rode across the land, the darkening landscape in the rain. . . .*

Café Trieste

CAFÉ TRIESTE, where I always had my amorous or celebratory espressos, is the café where writers have come since the Beat days. I spent many sweet hours here, dreaming of poetry and girls. The Trieste communicates by an underground passage with all the cafés of my adolescence and youth, Café Maria in Sibiu, the Capşa in Bucharest, the Figaro in New York.

Duc Nguyen

DUC NGUYEN comes from a bohemian café society too—that of Vietnam. He is an American radio commentator, like me. He comments and dreams, the way I do, about the curious nature of our split existence.

Duc honored me by inviting me to his house to meet his father, a poet and former South Vietnamese government official, who spent twelve years in a North Vietnamese prison.

Vietnam was the burning issue of my day when I came to America. A quarter of a century later it is still an open wound in America's psyche. These two men, father and son, are the bookends between which stretches the vast library of America's sorrows. Duc and Dad are not Americans but they have experienced the uniquely American drama of the generation gap.

I asked Mr. Nguyen to read one of the poems he wrote during the long years he spent in prison.

Duc's translation of his father's poem:

> *Dust falls*
> *Rotting with the passing time*
> *And drifting clouds in front of the prison window*
> *grieve over a betrayed goal*
> *Waking up in the morning I feel disconsolate*
> *about my homeland's misfortune.*

AC to Mr. Nguyen: *Would you ever consider going back to live in Vietnam?*

MR. NGUYEN: *I don't like to be back now. So I enjoy freedom. The freedom I was looking for a long time.*

AC: *How about you, Duc?*

DUC: *I think I'm ready to go back tomorrow. I mean, I feel very comfortable there. And I want to go back to Vietnam to be with friends, to tell them about my fears, my joys, whatever. And that kind of thing can only happen in Vietnam for me. But I know I can't walk down the street and say, you know, "Let's change the government now and move to a multiparty system." I'd be put in prison within ten seconds.*

AC: *Well, that seems to me a great price to pay just for being able to hang with your friends in a café.*

DUC: *I've never seen this as a new home. To me the word "home" means only one thing, and that means Vietnam.*

MR. NGUYEN: *I have suffered so many years under the dictatorial regime. So, I highly prize the value of freedom.*

The New Americans

I COULD never live in Romania again. I know I'm a full-fledged American, because I've been asked to help officiate at the swearing-in ceremony for new immigrants.

IMMIGRATION AND NATURALIZATION SERVICE OFFICIAL: *I will support and defend—*

CROWD: *I will support and defend—*

INS OFFICIAL: *—the Constitution and the laws of the United States of America.*

CROWD: *—the Constitution and the laws of the United States of America.*

INS OFFICIAL: *—against all enemies, foreign and domestic, so help me God.*

I never thought—in my wildest dreams—that I would one day share a podium with officials of the Immigration and Naturalization Service who gave me so much grief. Only in America could they be so casual about the past. Didn't anybody check my file?

Anxious faces from forty-one nations stood before me. "Ladies and gentlemen, welcome to the hollo-deck! The secret of capitalism is forgetting. The quicker you forget, the less you will suffer. On the other hand, if you choose not to forget, like the Native Americans or the Bruderhoff, you'll have a real tough time and you'll never be on TV unless I visit you—" That's what I wanted to tell them.

This is what I told them:

Immigration and Naturalization Service: Speech to the New Americans of 1992

HELLO, NEW AMERICANS!

Ladies and gentlemen, friends, and fellow citizens,

I am Yakov Smirnoff from Moscow, Russia, and I'm here to tell you that this country been very very good to me. I can have all the vodka I want.

No, I'm not really Yakov Smirnoff from Russia. I'm Andrei Codrescu from Romania, and this country has been very very good to me. I can have all the tzuica *I want but I won't because it's not good for my body.*

Romania was a Communist country when I was growing up (remember the Iron Curtain?). In school they told us that America was a bad place where the rich laughed in the face of the poor who went about begging in the streets. That America was a country where crime and racism made it dangerous to walk outside.

My grandmother, on the other hand, whispered to me that in America "dogs walk around with pretzels on their tails." Fat, healthy dogs. Big, hot pretzels. She also whispered that in America the "roads are paved with gold." That wasn't as good as the dogs with the pretzels—but she had to whisper because in Romania you could not say such things out loud.

I myself imagined America as the place where I could be a very famous writer who could say out loud all the things that would land me in jail in Romania.

When I came to America I found that the school and my grandmother were both wrong.

The rich didn't exactly laugh in the face of the poor but they didn't smile kindly either. The rich gave only reluctantly to help their fellow human beings and only after the government made them do it. Crime was as bad as they said it was. And racism was real. The melting pot of America was a boiling cauldron of prejudice.

And yes, in America some dogs not only walked around with pretzels on their tails but got their own burial plots in Hollywood. Some dogs inherited fortunes and were tended by human servants.

But the roads were not paved with gold. In fact, in 1992, certain roads are not paved at all because there isn't enough money to pave them with.

Yes, there are beggars and poor people and very rich people in America. But mostly there are in-between people, people who are neither rich nor poor, people who have nice houses or apartments with a little garden or a balcony, people who treat their dogs very nicely if they have dogs, people who (for the most part) let each other talk, laugh, and vote however they please. People who do not have to whisper. And the roads, whether in good shape or not, can take you somewhere else if you do not like where you are. America is a big country and you can move anywhere you want in it without having to show your passport.

Almost ten years ago I sat where you sit now and listened to a judge welcome me to America. "You are now Americans," the judge said. "You can keep your native customs, you can keep your wonderful cooking and your churches, but you are not Chinese, Haitians, Russians, or Romanians any longer. You cannot hold the interests of your old countries above those of your new country. You are now Americans."

The judge spoke the truth. But the judge did not mention how hard it is to keep your customs, your cooking, and your language alive. The judge did not mention the loneliness of having left friends and family behind. He did not mention the embarrassment of different manners, the trauma of simple exchanges and transactions. He did not mention the heartbreak of watching your children forget where they came from.

For me, this was all good. I came here when I was nineteen years old. My loneliness became a time to dream ambitious dreams, dreams of revenge and conquest, dreams of showing everyone that I was more than the skinny little foreigner with holes in his shoes who could not speak very good English.

I also used my embarrassment so as not to take myself so seriously. One time, in Detroit, I asked a bus driver: "Can I buy this bus?" I meant to say, "Can I ride this bus?" He pushed me away and said: "Go buy the next bus!"

I haven't bought that bus yet—but I just bought a car.

And as for the heartbreak of your children becoming American, that is inevitable. I was only a child myself when I came here but now I have children of my own. They are very American. They like to read books but they also play sports. In Romania you either read books or played sports. You couldn't do both. And my children, as American as they are, are very interested in where they come from. They are proud of it, in fact, because it makes them different.

And so—I would modify what the judge said to me ten years ago in this way:

"You must make an effort to keep your old customs and to make others admire them, you must use your native cooking to make new friends and to bring your community together; you must make an effort to support the community life of your fellow immigrants. You are still Chinese, Haitians, Russians, and Romanians, but you are also American, which means that you can be better Chinese, better Haitians and Russians and Romanians—better because you are living together with all of these other people and you can enrich each other through your differences. You are American now, which means that you must forget the hatreds and prejudices of your own past ... that if you are a Croatian American you cannot fight your Serbian American neighbor because that's what is going on in the old country. You cannot pass on to your children the prejudices and hatreds of the old country. You must always remember why you left your countries in the first place: because you were persecuted for your political beliefs, for your religious beliefs, or simply because you wanted to live a better material life. ... No matter. All those reasons are precisely why you must heal the wounds of the past. America is the place where you must deliberately forgo revenge if you are to go forward. You can be born again here, but like a baby you must cancel the pain that brought you here.

America was set up as a place to get away from the murderous sentimentalities of the old worlds—which does not mean that you must abandon or forget the beauties of your cultures. On the contrary. The greater and prouder the cultural difference you bring here the greater your success. America changes with every single new citizen. America in 1992 is not the America I came into in 1966. Today, Spanish is spoken almost as much as English, and millions of people from Asia, the Caribbean, and the Pacific have come since then, changing the flavor and look of the place, making America more colorful, spicier, more exciting.

The American poet Walt Whitman wrote in 1855:

I celebrate myself, and sing myself,
And what I assume you shall assume,
For every atom belonging to me as good belongs to you.

And so it is. Today's song may be a bit darker and more difficult but
it's still there.
America is an idea in our minds. Every generation of new immigrants
remakes America in the shape of what they imagine it to be.
It's your turn.

Land's End

I PARKED the car at the end of Golden Gate Park and walked on the
beach. It was a gray day, the color of thought. A mass of swirling
clouds, looking Chinese, moved over the bridge. The smell of eucalyp-
tus came wafting in. Hugely incompatible ingredients were thrown
into the boiling cauldron of this continent—and very little, thank God,
has actually melted in this vast melting pot: languages, people, habits,
cuisines, mores, customs, manners, and beliefs continue undaunted side
by side.

What keeps us together is precisely the awed awareness of our
differences—and the wondrous fact that we can exist in each other's
company and even—occasionally, and, alas, too rarely—love one another.

And there is something else, namely a force that belongs to the land
itself, a native American force that bids us seek the heavenly city
. . . pursue the illusory light of the spirit. Paradoxically, the most
materialistic country in the world is also the most spiritual. I, for one,
new American and even newer driver, am grateful to that native force.

"The land is an Indian thing." I believe that. But it's also a
Romanian thing.

We shed our skins as we move—
Why does she love us still?

Also by Andrei Codrescu

POETRY
Belligerence / Comrade Past and Mister Present / Selected Poems:
1970–1980 / Diapers on the Snow / Necrocorrida / For the Love of a Coat / The
Lady Painter / The Marriage of Insult and Injury / A Mote Suite for Jan and
Anselm / Grammar and Money / A Serious Morning / Secret Training / the,
here, what, where / The History of the Growth of Heaven / License to Carry a
Gun

FICTION
Monsieur Teste in America and Other Instances of Realism / The Repentance of
Lorraine / Why I Can't Talk on the Telephone

MEMOIRS
The Hole in the Flag / In America's Shoes / The Life and Times of an
Involuntary Genius

ESSAYS
The Disappearance of the Outside / Raised by Puppets Only to Be Killed by
Research / A Craving for Swan

TRANSLATION
At the Court of Yearning: The Poems of Lucian Blaga / For Max Jacob

WORKS EDITED
American Poetry Since 1970: Up Late / The Stiffest of the Corpse: An Exquisite
Corpse Reader / Exquisite Corpse: A Monthly Journal of Books and Ideas

Also by David Graham

Only in America
American Beauty

BILL CHURCH